W9-BZA-745

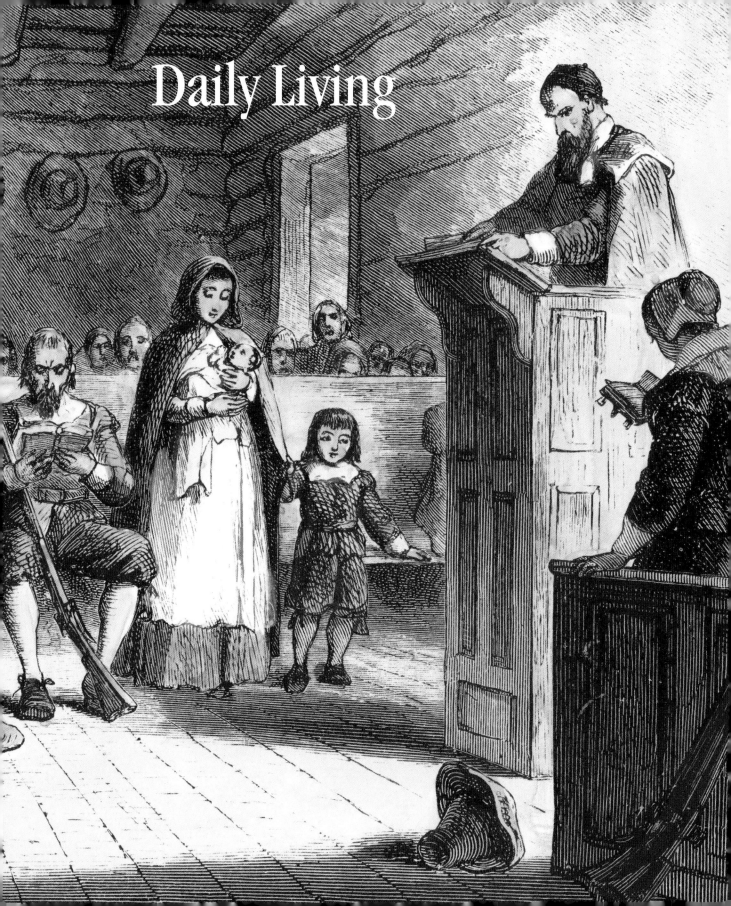

Daily Living

COLONIAL LIFE

Daily Living

Kathryn Hinds

Sharpe Focus
an imprint of M.E. Sharpe, Inc.

In memory of my grandmothers, Grace Hausknecht Lupton and Mildred Van Auken Fernquist.

Sharpe Focus
An imprint of M.E. Sharpe, Inc.
80 Business Park Drive
Armonk, NY 10504
www.mesharpe.com

ISBN: 978-0-7656-8110-2

Library of Congress Cataloging-in-Publication Data

Hinds, Kathryn, 1962-
  Daily living / Kathryn Hinds.
      p. cm. -- (Colonial life)
  Includes bibliographical references and index.
  ISBN 978-0-7656-8110-2 (hardcover : alk. paper)
  1. United States--Social life and customs--To 1775--Juvenile literature.
  2. Colonists--United States--Social life and customs--17th
  century--Juvenile literature. 3. Colonists--United States--Social life and
  customs--18th century--Juvenile literature. I. Title.

E162.H56 2008
973.2--dc22

                                                  2007007844

Editor: Peter Mavrikis
Program Coordinator: Cathleen Prisco
Production Manager: Laura Brengelman
Editorial Assistant: Alison Morretta
Design: Charles Davey LLC, Book Productions

Printed in Malaysia

9 8 7 6 5 4 3 2 1

Contents ❧

French fur traders in Port–Royal (now Annapolis Royal), Canada, brightened the winter of 1606–1607 with regular feasts held in the common room of their headquarters. The French were frequently joined by members of the Micmac tribe, with whom they had close ties.

CHAPTER ONE ❧
Varieties of Experience

THE EUROPEANS WHO COLONIZED NORTH AMERICA

came from many backgrounds and found themselves in many different situations. The first settlers were adventurers and pioneers, trying to make their home in an unfamiliar and often hostile land. Their children, as well as later arrivals, would generally have easier lives in established towns or villages. Yet as the colonies expanded, some settlers moved out to the frontiers, keeping the pioneer spirit alive as part of life in the New World. Where people lived—on the frontier, on a farm, on a seacoast, in a town—was just one of the factors that affected how they lived.

National Origins

Colonists came to North America from different nations, and from different regions within those nations. Even after several generations, these origins still influenced daily life in a variety of ways.

The main groups of early settlers were from Spain, Britain, and France. The Spanish colonized Central America, Mexico, the American Southwest, California, and Florida; the British occupied much of the east coast of what would become the United States; the French settled Quebec and areas around the St. Lawrence River, Great Lakes, and Mississippi River. There was also a Dutch colony in the Hudson River valley, in today's New York State, that included Manhattan and part of Long Island. The Dutch city of New Amsterdam on Manhattan Island was also home to Protestant colonists from Spain, Denmark, Italy, France, and what is now Belgium. And a small Swedish colony (whose residents were from Finland as well as Sweden) existed in Delaware. In addition, Spain, Britain, France, and the Netherlands all had settlements on the islands in the Caribbean Sea.

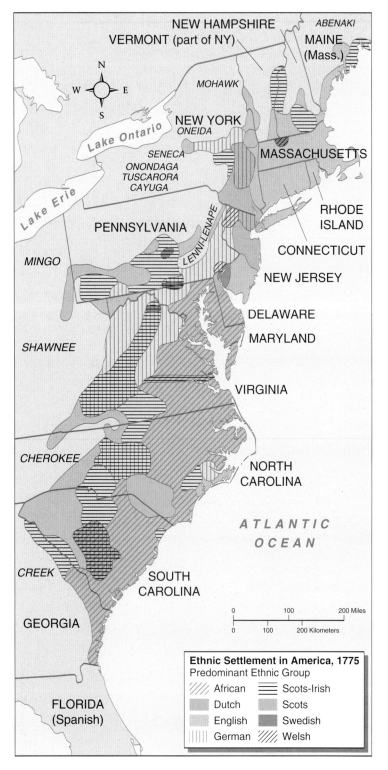

Ethnic Settlement in America, 1775
Predominant Ethnic Group

//// African
▨ Dutch
▦ English
||| German
═ Scots-Irish
▤ Scots
▨ Swedish
//// Welsh

Sweden kept its colony for less than twenty years before it was overcome by the Dutch colony in 1655. Nine years later, the Dutch settlements were taken over by the British. Britain gradually gained control of most of the French settlements, too.

When the French and Indian War ended in 1763, the only territory in North America that France held on to was in the Caribbean: Britain possessed Canada, and Louisiana, although it remained French in culture, was owned by Spain. At the same time, Spain ceded Florida to Britain, which had become the dominant colonial power in North America.

Britain's dominance meant that English law, customs, and language held sway in the non-Spanish colonies, but it did not mean that only the British lived there. Diversity was part of the American experience from the very beginning. Even among the British there were differ-

This map shows where various European ethnic groups, as well as Africans and Native Americans, were settled in the thirteen colonies around 1775.

ent ethnic groups—English, Welsh, and Scottish—and among these groups there were also various regional differences.

Other ethnic and national groups in the British colonies included Scots-Irish (from northern Ireland), Irish, Swiss, French, and Germans, along with the descendants of Dutch and Swedish settlers. In New York there was also a community of Portuguese Jews who had previously lived in Brazil. Jamestown had Polish and Italian glassmakers, and a group of Italian silk workers lived in Savannah, Georgia. In Massachusetts Bay, colonists from Denmark built and ran a sawmill.

Many settlements also had Native American residents, who lived at least part-time among the European settlers. Finally, the colonies became home to a large number of people of African origin, though few were willing immigrants—by the end of the colonial period, millions of Africans had been brought to North America as slaves.

Regional Differences

Colonists in North America found themselves in a land of diverse environments, from northeastern Canada with its icy winters to the Caribbean with its tropical climate. Most Spanish settlements were in hot and often dry areas. Some, like San Diego, were located along the Pacific coast; others were well inland, in Mexico and the American Southwest. Spanish St. Augustine, the first permanent European settlement in what would become the United States, was on the Atlantic coast of Florida.

The French were present in many regions, although a large number of their settlements, especially in places such as the Mississippi River valley, were little more than trading posts. The two major French cities were in very different environments: Quebec City on the St.

Britain forced thousands of French settlers to leave eastern Canada during the French and Indian War (1754–1763). Many of these exiled French Canadians found new homes in Louisiana.

Lawrence River in Canada and, far to the south, New Orleans on the Gulf of Mexico.

The early English colonies were established either on the Atlantic coast or on rivers a little way inland. Jamestown (Virginia), the first permanent English settlement, was in a marshy area on the James River near the opening of Chesapeake Bay. The second, Plymouth (Massachusetts), was on the sheltered bay formed by Cape Cod. Gradually, English colonial boundaries were pushed farther west. By the mid-1700s, the frontier lay along the Appalachian (app-ah-LAY-chun) mountain range, and pioneers were ready to seek lands beyond the mountains.

Environmental conditions varied widely through the colonies. Northern areas had much shorter growing seasons than did southern ones. In the far north, crops could not be grown at all, but there were many fur-bearing animals that could be hunted or trapped. Thick

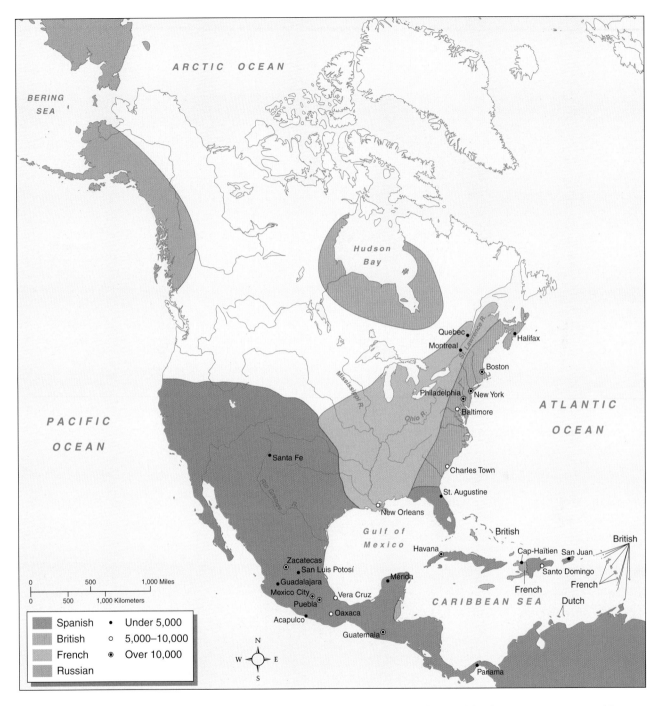

Most of early North America was rural. Cities, especially large ones, were few and far between, as seen on this map showing settlement patterns around 1750. Mexico City was the largest urban area in North America, with more than 100,000 people. The biggest city in the thirteen colonies was Philadelphia, with somewhat less than 20,000.

forests were common in the east; many areas of the southwest were desert, or close to it. People living along the Atlantic Ocean and the Gulf of Mexico often contended with fierce storms, including hurricanes. Heavy snows and freezing winter temperatures challenged northern colonists, while extreme heat and humidity in the summer could cause problems for those in the south.

Some colonists found the land and the weather in their part of the New World similar to Europe. Many others, though, were forced to significantly adapt their way of life in order to survive.

Religious Expectations

Many colonists came to North America with religious goals in mind. The most familiar example is the Pilgrims, who were known as Separatists because they wanted to separate from the Church of England, which they regarded as corrupt. Back home in England this was an illegal act, because the church was part of the state.

The oldest synagogue in the United States, the Touro Synagogue, was built in 1762 by the Jewish community of Newport, Rhode Island. It remains an active house of worship today.

Before coming to the New World in 1620, the Pilgrims spent a dozen years in the Netherlands, where church and state were separate. Although the Pilgrims appreciated the freedom to worship as they chose, they were reluctant to stay in the Netherlands—they cherished their English identity and did not want to become Dutch. Their daring plan to settle in North America offered them the opportunity to live in an English-speaking, English-culture community—and yet pursue their own religious ideas. The Pilgrims established Plymouth Colony in what is now the state of Massachusetts.

In 1630, ten years after the Pilgrims arrived in the New World, another group of English settlers founded the Massachusetts Bay Colony, with its center in Boston, about 40 miles (65 kilometers) north of Plymouth. The new colonists were Puritans, who wanted to purify the Church of England. They intended their new home to be a "city

Boston's town hall (the large building on the left) and main street were centers of colonial life in the mid-1700s.

When William Penn founded Pennsylvania, he worked hard to establish and maintain friendly relations with the Lenni Lenape (or Delaware) people, the Native Americans of the region.

on a hill" that would shine out as an example of righteousness. Within a few years Puritans were also settling in what is now Connecticut.

The Massachusetts Bay Puritans had no tolerance for any form of religion but their own. In addition, there was no division between religious and political authority—so anyone who disagreed with church authorities or teachings could be banished from the colony or punished in other ways. When Massachusetts Bay banished minister Roger Williams, he set out for lands west of Plymouth and founded Providence, the beginning of the colony of Rhode Island. Williams promoted the separation of religion and government, and Rhode Island became home to many different types of Protestant Christians as well as to a small community of Jews. Exiles from Massachusetts Bay also settled in New Hampshire, as did many other types of Protestants.

The most diverse and tolerant colonies were Pennsylvania and New Jersey. William Penn, the founder of Pennsylvania, was a member of the Religious Society of Friends, or Quakers, whose principles included nonviolence, social equality, and religious tolerance. Penn looked on his colony as a "holy experiment" in which these principles could be put into action, and he welcomed colonists of many faiths and nationalities. Neighboring New Jersey also had a large population of Quakers, and so welcomed similar diversity.

Many different Christian groups could be found in New York, too, where there was also a Jewish community in Manhattan. (Additional colonial Jewish communities could be found in Philadelphia; Savannah, Georgia; and South Carolina.) New York's colonists had come to North America mainly for nonreligious reasons—they tended to be more motivated by economic opportunity than by the desire for religious freedom. The same was true of nearly all of England's southern colonies.

Maryland, however, was founded by the Catholic nobleman Lord Baltimore as a refuge for English Catholics, who were a minority with limited rights in their homeland. Although it was settled by Catholics, the colony was open to non-Catholics, too. By the 1700s it had a Protestant majority—which then for many years denied freedom of worship to Catholics and persecuted them in other ways.

In the French and Spanish colonies, on the other hand, Catholicism was the official religion. (French Protestants, called Huguenots, settled in the English colonies, especially in Charleston, South Carolina, rather than in French territory.) Many priests and monks emigrated to the New World for the purpose of converting the native peoples to Christianity. The king of Spain, in fact, decreed in 1526 that every expedition to the Americas must include at least two priests.

In 1573, Spain declared that the main reason for colonization was to spread Christianity. Throughout Spanish America, priests and monks set up missions where they tried to convince the Indians to give up their traditional beliefs and adopt the Spanish way of life. Many of these missions, such as the one in Santa Fe, New Mexico, grew into thriving towns.

French mission settlements were not as widespread. The missionaries tended to travel out from bases in French towns, or to live for extended periods within Indian communities. They encouraged native parents to send their children to Quebec, or even to France, to live with French families and learn Christianity and European culture. In addition, Quebec City had a convent of nuns who were dedicated to educating both French and native girls.

Class and Gender Differences

Colonists' daily lives depended very much on how well off they were and what class they belonged to. More than half of all immigrants came to the British colonies as indentured servants. This meant that in return for the cost of the voyage, they had to serve a master for four to seven years. During this time indentured servants had no rights and could be treated as property—bought and sold, forbidden to marry, separated from family members, and beaten for even small offenses.

Their masters were supposed to provide them with food, clothing, and other necessities, but a great many indentured servants were ill fed, poorly clothed, and weak from overwork, hunger, and disease. Mistreated servants often ran away. If they were caught, however, not only could they be punished by whipping, but their period of servitude could be lengthened, sometimes even doubled.

Indentured servants were mainly from England in the 1600s and from Germany and Ireland in the 1700s. Some servants did not come to the New World willingly, but were rounded up from the streets and poorhouses of European cities. Others were convicted of crimes in Europe and sentenced to indentured servitude in the New World as punishment.

These servants often worked side by side with African laborers. The earliest Africans in Virginia and some other colonies may have been regarded as indentured servants and set free after several years. But slavery had been well established in the Caribbean and South America since the 1500s, and it did not take long for African and African American workers to be regarded as lifelong slaves.

Indentured servants could at least look forward to eventual freedom. In the first half of the 1600s, they could even expect to become landowners—perhaps not wealthy, but reasonably well

Ballad of an Indentured Servant ⌀

More than 75 percent of the English emigrants to Virginia in the 1600s were indentured servants—and not all of them came to the New World willingly. The following early American ballad, "The Trappan'd [Trapped] Maiden," is the lament of a young woman tricked—or possibly even kidnapped—into indentured servitude.

> Give ear unto a Maid, that lately was betray'd,
> > And sent into Virginny, O:
> In brief I shall declare, what I have suffer'd there,
> > When that I was weary, weary, weary, weary, O. . . .
>
> Five years served I, under Master Guy,
> > In the land of Virginny, O,
> Which made me for to know sorrow, grief and woe,
> > When that I was weary, weary, weary, weary, O. . . .
>
> I have played my part both at Plow and Cart,
> > In the land of Virginny, O;
> Billets from the Wood upon my back they load,
> > When that I am weary, weary, weary, weary, O. . . .
>
> Then let Maids beware, all by my ill-fare,
> > In the land of Virginny, O;
> Be sure to stay at home, for if you here do come,
> > You all will be weary, weary, weary, weary, O. . . .

Surviving a Hurricane ⊱

The following poem was written by Phillis Wheatley. Born in West Africa, she was brought to Boston as a slave in 1761, when she was about seven years old. A merchant purchased her to be a servant for his wife, but instead of teaching her domestic skills, the couple ended up teaching her reading, writing, the Bible, literature, and the Greek and Latin classics. Phillis Wheatley's book of poems was published in 1773, and later that year she was given her freedom.

To a Lady on her remarkable Preservation
in an Hurricane in North-Carolina

Though thou did'st hear the tempest from afar,
And felt'st the horrors of the wat'ry war,
To me unknown, yet on this peaceful shore
Methinks I hear the storm tumultuous roar....
The billows rave, the wind's fierce tyrant roars,
And with his thund'ring terrors shakes the shores:
Broken by waves the vessel's frame is rent,
And strows with planks the wat'ry element.
    But thee, Maria, a kind Nereid's* shield
Preserv'd from sinking, and thy form upheld....
    From tossing seas I welcome thee to land.
"Resign her, Nereid," 'twas thy God's command.
Thy spouse late buried, as thy fears conceiv'd,
Again returns, thy fears are all relieved:
Thy daughter blooming with superior grace
Again thou see'st, again thine arms embrace;
O come, and joyful show thy spouse his heir,
And what the blessings of maternal care!

* A Nereid was a sea goddess.

off, and able to participate in the colonial government. But as the colonies grew, so too did great differences in wealth and social class. Former indentured servants typically remained poor and landless. The more fortunate of these might become tenant farmers, living on and working someone else's land. The less fortunate became unskilled laborers, living in rented rooms, or even homeless beggars.

By the 1700s the poor were numerous and the wealthy few. But these few were very wealthy and powerful indeed, often living in large mansions on estates of thousands of acres. They controlled colonial trade and government institutions, enjoyed European luxuries, and had servants and slaves to work for them. Though making up only 1 to 5 percent of the population, this upper class typically owned at least half of all the land and wealth in a colony.

Between the extremes of rich and poor, a growing number of

people belonged to the "middling" class. These were small farmers, craftspeople, shopkeepers, and the like—the type of people we usually think of when we think of colonial America. Some were better off than others, and a number of them resented the fact that the very wealthy had so much control over government, taxation, and trade. But most lived in reasonable comfort, working hard and enjoying the fruits of their labors.

There was one more basic and essential factor that could impact daily life: whether a colonist was male or female. As in Europe, this would determine much about a person's life, starting in childhood. Gender affected everything from what people wore to what kind of work they might do to how much they might participate in decision making.

In all the colonies, it was felt that women and men had distinct roles to play and that men were always superior and should always be in charge. Actual conditions, though, especially in the early decades of a colony, meant that women and their work often enjoyed great respect—no colony, after all, could succeed without the contributions of all its members, male or female.

In this portrait drawn around 1770, Phillis Wheatley is shown working on one of her poems. She was the first published African American poet.

Transportation by water was crucial to settlement and trade in North America. Settlers sometimes dug canals to reach and connect the larger waterways they used. This view of Dutch New Amsterdam shows the canal that ran down the middle of Broad Street and led to the harbor. The canal was filled in in 1676, after Britain had taken over the city and renamed it New York.

CHAPTER TWO ❧
Basic Conditions

A WIDE RANGE OF FACTORS COULD

cause large differences in the experience of daily life for colonists. There were some conditions, though, that all colonists shared. For the earliest European immigrants, one overwhelmingly important circumstance was that they were facing an almost completely unknown new world. To them, it was an uncharted wilderness. They did not know the terrain or the climate; many of the plants and animals were unfamiliar. And they had only the vaguest notions about the natives of North America. In addition to all of this strangeness, colonists also had to cope with being virtually cut off from their European homelands and any friends and family members they had left behind. The fear, isolation, and homesickness must sometimes have been overwhelming.

Resources

Natural resources varied from region to region. Along the seacoasts and rivers, people had access to a wide variety of fish; marshes were abundant with ducks and other waterfowl; forests sheltered deer and wild turkeys. Some areas—mostly those colonized by Spain—had a wealth of precious metals. Other areas yielded wealth in the form of furs, timber, or tobacco. In much of North America, however, there were two resources that seemed especially plentiful to colonists: land and water.

The poet Anne Bradstreet was among the first English settlers of Massachusetts. She often suffered ill health but, as a devout Puritan, she turned sickness into an opportunity for religious experience, as in this poem addressed to God.

For Deliverance from a Fever

When sorrows had begirt me round,
And pains within and out,
When in my flesh no part was found,
Then didst Thou rid me out.
My burning flesh in sweat did boil,
My aching head did break,
From side to side for ease I toil,
So faint I could not speak.
Beclouded was my soul with fear
Of Thy displeasure sore,
Nor could I read my evidence
Which oft I read before.
"Hide not Thy face from me!" I cried,
"From burnings keep my soul.
Thou know'st my heart, and hast me tried;
I on Thy mercies roll."
"O heal my soul," Thou know'st I said,
"Though flesh consume to nought,
What though in dust it shall be laid,
To glory t' shall be brought."
Thou heard'st, Thy rod Thou didst remove
And spared my body frail,
Thou show'st to me Thy tender love,
My heart no more might quail.
O, praises to my mighty God,
Praise to my Lord, I say,
Who hath redeemed my soul from pit,
Praises to him for aye.

When the Spanish arrived in Mexico and Central America in the 1500s, they encountered the fields, cities, and villages of the Aztec and Maya peoples; the region was far from an empty wilderness. But in the 1600s and farther north, French, Dutch, Swedish, and English colonists found a different situation. By this time huge numbers of the native population had been killed by diseases brought by the Spanish and other early European explorers, traders, and fishermen. Where there had once been thriving communities, many areas were depopulated. For example, when the Pilgrims arrived in Massachusetts and began looking for places to settle, they found a number of deserted Native American villages and fields, as well as the unburied skeletons of disease victims.

In addition, Europeans were not familiar with the way native peoples used the land. To take the Pilgrims as an example again, when they at last chose their

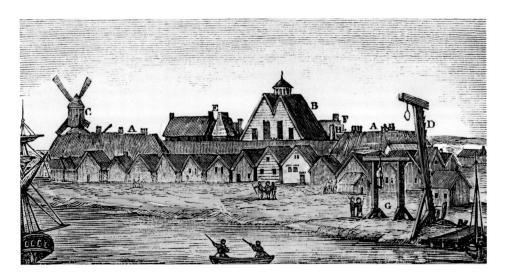

This is a view of the Dutch town of New Amsterdam in 1659. The pillory and gallows, where crimes were punished, were located outside the town's wall.

colony's location, they thought it was uninhabited. Even though the site had been cleared, they found no settlements there and scarcely saw an Indian in the vicinity during their first few months in Plymouth. Then during the summer, at least a dozen members of the Pokanoket (poh-kuh-NOH-ket) tribe came to Plymouth Harbor to catch lobsters, as they had been doing every summer for years, even generations. Like many Indians of eastern North America, they used different parts of their territory in different ways at different times of year, moving between villages, fields, hunting grounds, and fishing grounds according to their needs and the seasons. And when the fields were worn out, the people would leave them and clear new fields, perhaps even moving their whole village. Because of these practices, much of the land occupied by native peoples appeared uninhabited to the colonists.

The seeming availability of so much land was an overwhelming temptation to Europeans. Wealthy investors saw an opportunity to get wealthier. Landless gentlemen, as well as many poor people, saw an opportunity to become property owners. Religious dissenters saw an opportunity to live the way they wanted without being persecuted or distracted by the rest of society. All kinds of people saw an opportunity to start over in a new place.

What was more, the people who explored and settled along the Atlantic and Gulf coasts found countless streams and rivers that they could follow into the interior of the continent. These waterways were the earliest colonial "roads," leading to further exploration and settlement. As the colonists ventured up the rivers, they found that many of them flowed through wide and extremely fertile valleys—perfect farmland.

The New World's springs, creeks, and rivers ensured the good water supplies necessary for any settlement. And transportation by water allowed trade to thrive between coastal port cities and inland towns, farms, and trading posts. Moreover, many of the watercourses were fast running (much more so than in England), making them ideal for powering gristmills for grinding grain and sawmills for turning the plentiful trees into usable lumber.

Technology, Communications, and Transportation

Like Europe during the same period, the North American colonies were at a preindustrial level of technology. They had few machines or mechanical devices to make their work easier. The tools they did have ran mainly on the muscle power of people or animals. The main exceptions to this were the water-powered mills already mentioned and, less commonly, windmills, generally used for grinding grain.

Other kinds of mills employed animals to turn the mill wheels, which might grind bark (used for treating leather, dying cloth, and making ink) or tobacco. Fulling mills, which pounded woolen cloth to thicken it, sometimes ran on water power but usually ran on animal power.

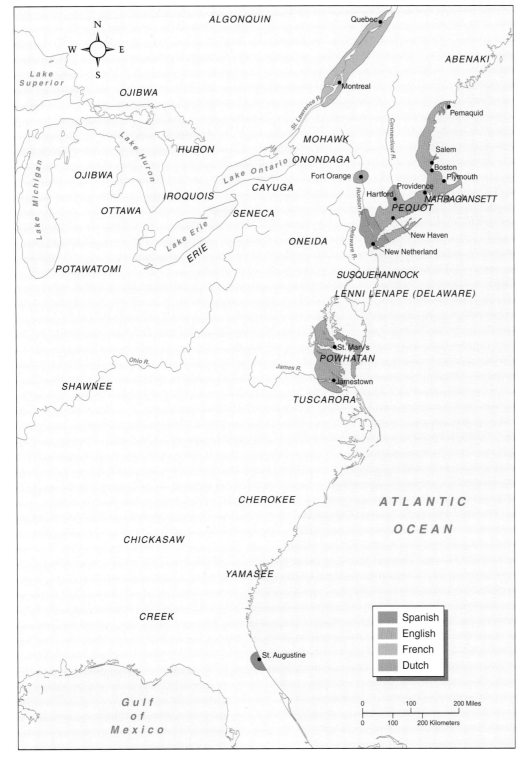

In 1650, Europeans occupied only a small part of eastern North America. There were no more than 50,000 Europeans and Africans in the British colonies, while the native peoples were numerous and their nations spread across the continent.

Another machine that became important to colonists was the printing press. The first one in the New World was set up in Mexico City in 1539. The first printing press in the British colonies was set up by Elizabeth Glover and Stephen Daye in Cambridge, Massachusetts, in 1638. There were not many printers in the colonies, since the type fonts and most of the presses had to be brought over from Europe. And there was only a small colonial market for finely printed books, maps, and the like—these, too, were usually imported. But the printers in the colonies turned out many inexpensive publications such as newspapers, almanacs, and pamphlets, which served local communities and helped keep colonists informed of current events and ideas.

A printer operates the first printing press in British North America. This first press was established in Cambridge, Massachusetts, in 1638.

Communication was a challenge in the New World, especially at first. There were large distances between colonies, which were also separated from one another by forests or other natural barriers. In addition, there were usually Native American settlements between one colony and another, and many of the native peoples were hostile toward the Europeans.

Communication between colonies and their mother countries was even more difficult. On the fastest route and in the best conditions, it took seven weeks to sail from Britain to the colonies. The prevailing winds made the trip in the other direction shorter, but if a colonist wrote a letter to someone in Europe, it would still take more than two months to get an answer.

The most complex technology of the colonial period was put to work in the building of ships, which were essential to the establishment and survival of colonies. Ships were the only way to reach North America, and they were the best way for colonies to communicate and trade with one another. Away from the port cities, colonists' transportation needs could be served by a variety of smaller vessels, such as barges, ferries, and birch bark or dugout canoes copied from those used by neighboring Indians.

A canoe was the only craft that most colonists, who did not have seamen's training, could operate. So for everyday travel—to market, to church, to visit friends— people either walked or rode horses. Horses did not become common, though, especially in New England, until after 1650. Early in the next century, coaches and carriages began to become available to wealthy colonists. These vehicles were status symbols, most suited for use on the streets of towns. By the mid-1700s, however, stagecoaches were running between some of the main cities in the British colonies.

This model canoe, from 1803, is a miniature version of the birch bark canoes that were used by Native Americans and colonists alike.

Around this time, too, the first Conestoga, or covered, wagons appeared. Introduced by German farmers in Pennsylvania, Conestogas were developed especially to bring agricultural products to market. The wagons were much roomier than previous designs had been, and the cloth cover protected produce from the elements during what could be a journey of several days. The practical design of Conestoga wagons would make them the favorite vehicle of generations of American pioneers.

The Intellectual Climate

Although colonists came from a variety of national, ethnic, and religious backgrounds, there were things that nearly all of them shared in terms of knowledge and ideas. This period, often known as the Age of Enlightenment, witnessed the beginnings of much of modern science. Great thinkers of the time, from Isaac Newton to Benjamin Franklin, celebrated the powers of human reason. But as yet, scientific explanations for many aspects of life were unknown or little understood.

Most colonists held to various old beliefs and practices that we would consider superstitious, although specific superstitions could differ from group to group and place to place. For example, many German colonists believed that they could guarantee the health of a newly bought pig by backing it into its pen, while settlers near the Appalachian Mountains would take a new baby out to make a footprint in the first snow as a way to prevent an illness known as croup.

It was very common to observe the heavens for signs of various kinds. Comets, meteor showers, the northern lights—to some these were warnings from God, to others they indicated good or bad luck for the person seeing them. The moon was watched especially closely: Since it was known to affect the tides, it was also thought to affect other parts of nature, especially the soil. Farm tasks were often done according to the moon's cycle. For example, the dark of the moon was a good time to plant root crops (such as carrots and turnips) but a bad time to pick apples (which would rot, no matter how well they were stored after picking).

Daily life was also affected by the state of knowledge about hygiene and sanitation. Many people believed that bathing was harmful

Missing the Old World ❧

Many colonists came to North America filled with hope for a better life. Yet even when they found it, they might never stop missing their native land—and sometimes they passed this feeling on to their children, too. Here is a 1725 letter from a young man named John Jones, who was born in Pennsylvania to parents who had emigrated from Wales. Jones's letter was written in Welsh to a relative back in Wales, and it is full of homesickness and nostalgia for that country.

I have heard my father speak much about old Wales. . . . I remember him frequently mentioning such places as Llanycil, Llanwchllyn, Llangwm, Bala, . . . and many others.

It is probably uninteresting to you to hear these names of places; but it affords me great delight even to think of them, although I do not know what kind of places they are; and indeed I long much to see them, having heard my father and mother so often speak in the most affectionate manner of the kind-hearted and innocent old people who lived in them, most of whom are now gone to their long home.

Frequently during long winter evenings, would they in merry mood prolong their conversation about their native land till midnight; and even after they had retired to rest, they would sometimes fondly recall to each other's recollection some man, or hill, house, or rock.

Really I can scarcely express in words how delighted this harmless old couple were to talk of their old habitations, their fathers and mothers, brothers and sisters, having been now twenty-four years in a distant and foreign land, without even the hope of seeing them more.

because it would strip off oils that kept the skin healthy. Bathing also required a lot of hard work, since water had to be fetched and heated one bucketful at a time. In addition, the most common kind of soap (made from woodash lye and animal fat) was extremely harsh, so it was really only suitable for laundry and household cleaning. In addition, bathtubs were not widely available or easily affordable for most of the colonial period.

This leaflet written by a Boston minister suggested that during outbreaks of smallpox or measles people could stay healthy by avoiding the "open Air." It also prescribed porridge, boiled apples, milk, and a little weak beer instead of meat and wine, which were thought to possess "a hot quality" that might encourage infection.

A BRIEF RULE

To guide the Common People of

NEW-ENGLAND

How to order themselves and theirs in the

Small Pocks, or Measels.

The small Pox (whose nature and cure the Measels follow) is a disease in the blood, endeavouring to recover a new form and state.

2. This nature attempts---1. By Separation of the impure from the pure, thrusting it out from the Veins to the Flesh.---2. By driving out the impure from the Flesh to the Skin.

3. The first Separation is done in the first four dayes by a Feaverish boyling (Ebullition of the Blood, laying down the impurities in the Fleshy parts which kindly effected the Feaverish tumult is calmed.

4. The second Separation from the Flesh to the Skin, or Superficies is done through the rest of the time of the disease.

A Friend, Reader to thy Welfare,

Thomas Thacher.

21. 11. 167⅞.

BOSTON, Printed and sold by John Foster. 1677

People were dirty, and so were their settlements. Trash was just swept or dumped outside—into the yard in rural areas, into the streets in towns. Chamber pots, too, were usually emptied right outside the house. As in Europe, people in the colonies regarded garbage as a nuisance, and they knew there was some connection with ill health—but they thought it was the bad smells that caused disease, not bacteria or viruses that bred in trash and sewage. Early on, the main way of handling garbage was to let pigs and goats roam free and eat it; crows and turkey buzzards—native scavengers—also helped out. By the end of the 1600s, though, a few cities had hired garbage collectors and street cleaners.

No one knew about germs yet. Most people, even doctors, did not understand that specific diseases had specific causes. One long-accepted theory held that all disease resulted from an imbalance in bodily fluids known as humors. Many Puritans believed that ill health (along with all other misfortunes) was a punishment from God or a sign of his displeasure. Some people thought that sickness could be caused by witches and their spells. Depending on the beliefs they held, colonists took steps to deal with all these possibilities, from regular bloodletting to keep the humors in balance, to vigorously punishing community members who did not live according to the Bible, to decorating the outside of houses with symbols meant to keep witches away.

Many people, though, were learning the medicinal properties of native plants and using them to treat health conditions without worrying about supernatural causes or medical theories. This kind of practical approach to knowledge would soon become one of the hallmarks of the way of life in the North American colonies.

Dutch family members, including a pet cat, gather around a fireplace in their New Netherland home.

CHAPTER THREE ❧
The Family and the Stages of Life

MOST OF THE EARLIEST COLONISTS—

Spanish conquistadores and priests, French trappers, and the founders of Jamestown—came to North America as single men. Women soon joined them. For example, Columbus brought thirty Spanish women with him to the Caribbean island of Hispaniola in 1498. Two English women joined the Jamestown settlers in 1608, followed by twenty the next year; a few children accompanied them. Ten years later, a sea captain brought around a hundred single women to Virginia to become the wives of men who reimbursed the captain for the women's passage.

Starting with the Pilgrims, more and more immigrants arrived in family groups. Single people generally came to the colonies as servants who were either already working for a family or soon became attached to one through indenture.

The single-family household quickly became the basic unit of colonial society. This household was home to a father, mother, and their children, and might also include an occasional unmarried, disabled, or elderly relative. In a craftsman's household there would generally be an apprentice or two, and well-off people had servants or slaves living in their home. In nearly all families, the head of the household was the father, who had the ultimate responsibility for everyone else's work, behavior, and well-being—physically, financially, and spiritually.

Birth and Infancy

It is very common to read of colonial families having a large number of children—Benjamin Franklin, for example, had sixteen siblings. But most households seem to have been about half that size, or smaller. Because of diseases and difficult conditions, it was rare for all the children born into a family to survive to adulthood. In seventeenth-century New England, one out of ten babies died before they were a year old. In the southern colonies during the same period, the infant death rate was almost 25 percent (one out of four babies), and another 25 percent would die before reaching the age of twenty.

This wicker cradle is said to have been brought from the Netherlands by a Pilgrim couple, Susanna and William White, who were expecting a child. Their son, Peregrine (the name means "pilgrim"), was born aboard the Mayflower as it lay at anchor off the Massachusetts coast in November 1620.

Nearly all babies were born at home. Usually a midwife would assist with the birth; if one was not available, a female relative or neighbor might help. Most midwives were women, but during the 1700s some male doctors also began delivering babies. No matter who was at the birth, though, it could be a dangerous time, especially for the mother. Complications of pregnancy and childbirth were the leading causes of death among colonial women—in New England, one out of five women died in childbirth, and the figure was even higher in the south. Many children, therefore, were raised by a stepmother.

If the mother lived, she almost always nursed her baby herself, usually for about two years. If she died, a wet nurse would be found—or, if necessary, the baby could be given goat's or cow's milk through a "baby bottle" made out of a cow's horn. In a wealthy southern family, though, a baby might be nursed by a slave woman, even if the mother was alive and well.

During the seventeenth century, it was very common to keep babies tightly wrapped in cloth bands called swaddling. The swaddling kept them warm, and it also kept their arms and legs straight and unmoving, which parents thought would make the limbs form properly. Many parents never allowed their children to crawl—it was believed to be too animal-like. Instead, when babies were six to nine months old, they were released from swaddling and put into a standing stool. Sometimes made from a hollowed-out log, this device held the child in a standing position and prevented much moving about. It also kept the child up off the floor, which could be dirty and cold. When children were ready to start walking, they were put into a walking stool, a wooden frame with wheels—the colonial version of a walker.

By the mid-1700s, Enlightenment ideas about child rearing were influencing many colonial parents. English philosopher John Locke's *Some Thoughts Concerning Education* (1693), a popular book on both sides of the Atlantic, discouraged swaddling and suggested that babies and young children wear loose, simple clothing. Locke also said that there was nothing wrong with allowing babies to crawl before they walked, and he was one of the first to recommend educational toys and learning through play.

Childhood

Puritans believed that all human beings were naturally sinful, and that they were born into this sinful state. For this reason, children were supervised and disciplined very strictly so that they would not give in to their own wills and desires; they ought to have no spirit of independence. Children were taught to obey their parents and others in authority absolutely and to show respect at all times. For example, they had to stand up and bow whenever their parents came near. Punishment for stubbornness and disobedience could be severe, as is demonstrated by the Puritan proverb "Better whipped than damned" —disobedience to parents was seen as a form of disobedience to God.

In contrast, by the early 1700s Quakers tended to believe that young children were in a natural state of innocence and were unable to sin until they became old enough to understand their actions. Parents tended to discipline children more through rewards for good behavior than punishment for bad and to reason with children as they grew older. Corporal punishment (beating, whipping, and so on) was very rare; many Quakers believed it violated their principles of nonviolence. In general, Quakers tried to provide a very protected, controlled environment for their children to grow up in, and they taught children from a young age to both respect and serve their community.

A Massachusetts girl stitched this sampler in the 1700s.

In spite of their sternness, Puritan parents normally loved their children very much, but they were discouraged from showing much affection. Quaker parents tended to be more openly loving, and Dutch colonists were even more so. So were settlers in the southern Appalachian frontier areas, who lavished their young children with attention and endearments. But corporal punishment, though frowned on, was often used by these "backcountry" parents as well.

Many frontier families also treated even the youngest children very differently depending on their sex. Little girls were taught to be obedient, hard working, patient, and self-sacrificing, while little boys were encouraged to be aggressive and independent and were frequently allowed to get their own way in everything. Virginia parents were also very permissive toward their male children, but, at least in the upper classes, they taught both boys and girls to behave as self-disciplined and well-mannered gentlemen and gentlewomen.

Wherever and however they were raised, children enjoyed various toys and games, although, depending on circumstances, some had more toys and playtime than did others. Colonial toys included rattles, alphabet blocks, balls, marbles, tops, whistles, drums, dolls and doll furniture, miniature tea sets, toy animals, toy carriages, and kites. Country children made many of their own toys from materials found in woods, fields, or farmyards—daisy chains and cornhusk dolls, for example. And imagination could easily turn a bit of bark floated on a creek into a boat or a sturdy stick into a hobbyhorse.

Baby rattles of silver and coral, like this one, were common among wealthy families in the British colonies during the 1600s and 1700s.

For games, there were versions of tag, hide-and-seek, leapfrog, blindman's buff, ring around the rosy, cat's cradle, badminton, and hopscotch. There were a variety of ball games, too, including a form of football as well as cricket and other ancestors of baseball. Children also enjoyed playing with pets—the Pilgrims had brought two dogs with them, and cats were probably on board almost every ship, where they kept rats and mice under control. They would continue this helpful work on colonial farms.

Childhood was brief, and rarely carefree. There were many dangers for children; in addition to diseases and poor conditions, to which children were especially vulnerable, there was the risk of accidents. Colonial homesteads were not "childproofed," and there were numerous cases of children being injured or killed by falling into open fireplaces or wells. Children might also experience loss, grief, and other hardships when siblings, parents, or other relatives died. The greatest hardships and sorrows were suffered by slave children, who could be sold away from their parents to endure lives of hard work and abuse from a very young age.

A Letter from a Schoolboy ๛

This letter was written in October 1752 by twelve-year-old John Ten Broeck to his father in Albany, New York, when John was away at boarding school in Connecticut. The Ten Broecks were descendants of some of New York's original Dutch colonists.

Honored Father,

These few lines come to let you know that I am in a good state of health and I hope this may find you also. I have found all the things in my trunk but I must have a pair of shoes. And mama please to send me some chestnuts and some walnuts; you please to send me a slate, and some pencils, and please to send me some smoked beef. . . . You please to send me a pair of Indian shoes. You please to send me some dried corn. My duty to Father and Mother and Sister and to all friends.

I am your dutiful son,

John Ten Broeck

Education

All colonial children received some form of education, even if it was just instruction in how to do their work. In many families, children began helping with farmwork and household chores as early as age three, learning by doing. A few years later, a boy would probably be given a jackknife—an important tool—and, soon after that, a bow and arrows or a gun, so that he could begin learning how to hunt and to prepare for service in the colonial militia.

Early on, too, parents started teaching their children manners and morals. Dutch children usually received their first instruction from their mothers, but among English colonists this was generally the father's responsibility. It was also most common for fathers to teach their children to read, write, and do at least simple math.

Not all children received this basic education, though. One scholar estimates that around 1700, only 69 percent of white males in New England, and 62 percent in Virginia, were literate. Another scholar estimates that around 1775 in the Middle Atlantic colonies (New York, Pennsylvania, Delaware, and New Jersey), 65 percent of men and 40 percent of women could read. Most slaves were not given the opportunity to learn to read; in some colonies, it was against the law to teach them to do so.

A relatively small number of colonial children got their basic education at school. In French and Spanish colonies, schools were run by the church. Generally they were part of missions, so most of the students were Native Americans whom the priests, monks, or nuns hoped to convert to Christianity. For Dutch colonists, too, education was closely linked with the church; the schools in Dutch New York were what we would call parochial schools. In New England, schools were not so directly run by churches, but they were still driven by religious ideals, for the Puritans believed that the most important goals of education were to enable people to read the Bible and to learn obedience to God.

By the mid-1600s, many New England towns had primary schools, and Boston even had a grammar school, a secondary school where boys could study Latin and other advanced subjects. But in rural areas it was harder to set up schools. Sometimes a local woman ran what was called a dame school, where she taught reading and writing in her home, usually just in the winter, when children were not needed to do farmwork. In the south people lived on widely separated plantations and farmsteads, so education was even more of a challenge. For anything beyond the basics, most wealthy families hired live-in tutors for their children. Some southern towns, though, had private academies to teach Latin and ancient history to boys and refined manners to girls.

A grandmother helps her grandson with his lessons. She uses one of her knitting needles to point out scenes from the Bible depicted on the tiles that surround the fireplace.

To learn to read, students often used a hornbook, a paddle-shaped piece of wood that held a sheet of parchment with the alphabet on it. Some primers, or basic reading books, were also available, but the Bible was usually the main textbook. Girls would practice both the alphabet and sewing skills by making samplers, which they typically embroidered with the alphabet; a Bible verse, short poem, or moral saying; and pictures of birds, flowers, or household scenes.

By the 1750s, many colonists wanted their children, especially their sons, to have a practical education, with instruction in subjects such as math, science, modern languages, business, and, in coastal cities, navigation. This kind of practical education was offered in the Philadelphia Academy (founded by, among others, Benjamin Franklin) and similar schools. They were only for boys at first, but many then added "female departments." Later, there were separate "female academies," where girls learned art, music, dancing, embroidery, and sewing as well as some academic subjects.

This was the most advanced education girls were likely to get, but some boys could go on to higher education. Some went to Europe to study, but by 1770 there were eight colleges in the British colonies. (There was also a college in Quebec City, founded in 1635.) Most of these schools focused on training young men to be ministers, but their education was also good preparation for careers in law, business, or public service.

Many young men—and a few young women—prepared for their careers by becoming apprentices. Apprenticeships for girls were usually in midwifery or in dressmaking and related trades, while boys had a much wider range of jobs open to them: silversmith, printer, blacksmith, tanner, glassblower, shipwright, shoemaker, cabinetmaker, and so on. An apprentice worked for a master for five to eight years, often bound by an indenture. In return for apprentices' labor,

Benjamin Franklin was much more than an elder statesman. He was also a printer, author, diplomat, scientist, and inventor. His inventions include bifocals, the lightning rod, and the Franklin stove. This painting was completed by Charles Willson Peale in 1789, one year before Franklin's death.

Young Ben Franklin ✑

Benjamin Franklin was born in Boston in 1706. His father, who made candles and soap for a living, was a devout Puritan who believed in giving one-tenth of his income to the church. Since Ben was his tenth child, he decided to have him educated for a career in the church. He taught him to read, then sent him off to school at the age of eight. Ben's best subject was writing, but he did not do very well in math. And as it turned out, he could only stay in school for two years—after that, his father could not afford the fees anymore.

Ben spent the next two years helping in his father's shop. He cut candle wicks, poured hot wax into molds, and ran errands. He hated it. When he was twelve, he told his father he wanted to go to sea. His father did not approve of this plan, but he knew that Ben would be unhappy making soap and candles for the rest of his life. So he sent him to be an apprentice to his older brother James, a printer.

Printing was work that Ben quickly came to enjoy, and he was good at it. Soon he could set type and run the press without his brother's supervision, and in 1721 the two of them began publishing a newspaper. Ben, a voracious reader, also started writing pieces of his own, which he submitted to the paper under the name Silence Dogood. James loved these clever articles—until he found out they were written by his little brother. Jealous of Ben's talent and skill, James began to beat him. So in 1723, Ben left Boston and ran away to Philadelphia.

Ben was seventeen years old now, and although he had almost no money and had not officially finished his apprenticeship, his skills and personality soon enabled him to get a job with a printer. The next step was to open his own print shop. After several years of working for other printers, in both Philadelphia and London, he was finally able to do so in 1730, at the age of twenty-four. Two years later he began writing and publishing *Poor Richard's Almanack*, which quickly became popular for its useful information, homespun proverbs, and funny stories. Benjamin Franklin was well on his way to becoming one of the most famous and influential people in America.

masters gave them housing, food, and training in their craft or trade. If all went well, at the end of the apprenticeship the young person would be able to set up in business for himself or herself.

In New England and Virginia formal apprenticeships were somewhat rare, but it was common for parents to send their children to live with other families almost as foster children, to be educated and to get some experience of life away from home. Probably the majority of colonial children, though, learned their adult roles mainly by working with and imitating their parents, in whose footsteps they would follow as farmers and housewives.

Courtship and Marriage

In most of the British colonies, people waited till about their mid-twenties to get married; usually the husband was at least a few years older than the wife. Different groups of colonists had different beliefs about what should happen before a couple married. Both bride and groom should consent to the marriage, and parental consent was also necessary. Among well-off families in Virginia, parents might play a large role in arranging the marriage, and there could be lengthy negotiations about the marriage contract and the amount of land and property each person would bring into the union. The bride and groom were usually not expected to love each other before the wedding, although everyone hoped that love would grow between them afterward.

Quakers, on the other hand, believed that marriage should unite "sweethearts" (a favorite Quaker term), although they expected the love between a couple to be more spiritual than romantic. They also had strict rules against marrying non-Quakers. Engagement was a long process that involved the entire community; all its members needed to consent to the marriage.

New England Puritans gather for a home wedding. The bride and groom stand holding hands in front of the magistrate (right), who performs the ceremony.

By modern standards, the most romantic colonists may have been the Puritans, who often used the phrase "falling in love" to describe the bond between couples and believed that it was essential for a man and a woman to be in love before marriage. For this reason Puritans promoted a period of courtship during which the couple could spend time together to make sure they really did love each other.

To give the couple some privacy and at the same time make sure their behavior remained righteous and respectable, Puritans came up with some helpful devices. One was the courting stick, a tube at least six feet (1.8 meters) long with a trumpetlike bell at each end. Through this, a man and woman could speak quietly to each other without touching and with family members in the same room to supervise. When the courtship got a little further along, the couple might "bundle," an old European custom that became very popular in New England. Bundling meant that the couple spent the night together in bed, tightly wrapped up in a blanket with a board between them. Sometimes the woman also wore a tight bundling stocking that went over both her legs.

For Puritans and Dutch colonists, marriage was a civil contract, not a religious ceremony, so their marriages were performed by magistrates rather than ministers. Quakers did not have ministers at all. Their weddings took place at meetings of the local community without ceremony: The bride and groom simply declared their wish to marry and made promises to each other in their own words. Settlers in the backcountry, who might live far from a church, often had informal marriage ceremonies. But even if all they did was publicly declare themselves as husband and wife, the event was usually surrounded by an array of traditional customs.

Members of the Church of England, on the other hand, had fairly elaborate wedding services, at home or in church, that followed a standard form and were performed by clergymen. Sometimes these couples also participated in the folk ceremony of jumping over a broomstick, a very old marriage rite from England. Slaves belonging to these families picked up this custom, and jumping the broom became a common wedding ceremony among African Americans, especially since legal and church weddings were not allowed for slaves.

Nearly all colonial weddings were celebrated with some kind of festivities, the type and amount depending on the family's wealth, religious beliefs, and cultural customs. Backcountry weddings, for example, generally included a lot of dancing and passing around bottles of whiskey. Wealthy Virginians threw fancy wedding balls and invited dozens of guests for days of feasting and merrymaking. On the other hand, Puritans believed that dancing and excessive eating and drinking were sinful, so they celebrated with a modest dinner and wedding cake.

Old Age

During the seventeenth century, a Virginian who reached the age of twenty could expect to live to be forty-five or so. New Englanders (especially men, who did not have to face the dangers of childbirth) could look forward to living into their sixties. The difference was caused by climate and environment. In the south, heat, humidity, swamps, and slow-moving streams created ideal conditions for malaria and other diseases. Weakened by disease, more women died in childbirth, too. As a result, few southern children reached adulthood without losing one or both parents (not to mention several siblings), and it was very unusual to have living grandparents. "Blended families"—with stepparents and stepsiblings—were common.

For the most part, elderly people in the colonies enjoyed a great deal of respect; they were looked on as elders whose knowledge and advice were of high value to the community. This was especially true among the Puritans, who believed that reaching old age was a sign of God's favor. The elderly were routinely given the best seats in church and at town meetings. Younger people respectfully addressed an old man as "Grandsire" and an old woman as "Gran'mam." High offices—such as governor of Massachusetts and president of Harvard College—were rarely held by men younger than sixty. Elderly men were generally obeyed without question, and there were many folktales—and some actual historical events—that featured "grey champions," aged men who took up arms to defend their communities in times of emergency.

William Goffe was known as a "grey champion." New England legend tells how he rallied the people of Hadley, Massachusetts, to defend themselves during the Native American uprising known as King Philip's War (1675–1676).

This bedroom of a wealthy eighteenth–century South Carolina family was luxuriously furnished with a canopied bed, rugs imported from Turkey or Persia, and a tall chest of drawers brought from England.

CHAPTER FOUR ❧
The Household

WE GENERALLY THINK OF THE COLONIAL settlements of North America in terms of towns and villages, farms and plantations—and these were the homes of most settlers. But before we take a closer look at them, we should remember that there were other living situations for colonists. Some were soldiers, housed in barracks inside forts. Others were priests, monks, or nuns who lived in monasteries or missions. Missions were also home to servants and to Native Americans who were learning about Christian and European beliefs and ways of life. Other Europeans in the colonies, such as French trappers, lived in native settlements at least part of the time. There were also trading posts; some of these grew into towns, while others remained just a few buildings surrounded by a wooden stockade.

Types of Houses

Colonial houses were built in a variety of styles. Especially during the early years, new settlers often built temporary structures so that they would have shelter while they constructed more substantial housing. One sort of temporary home was a cave dug into a bank or low cliff; this was common around Philadelphia for a time. The first home for colonists in both Virginia and New England was sometimes a rectangular hole in the ground; around seven feet (2.1 meters) deep, it would be lined and roofed with logs or planks. Other settlers built their own versions of native dwellings, using bark or animal skins to cover hut-like structures known as "English wigwams."

When settlers began to construct more permanent dwellings, they built in the style of their mother country as much as possible, but also adapted to

The Tate house was built in 1755 near what is now Portland, Maine. It was home to a wealthy British naval officer, Captain George Tate, and his family. Tate oversaw the production of masts for navy ships from this spacious house. It also included an elegant parlor where the Tates held dances and dinner parties.

their new land's conditions and available materials. Early English colonists typically built their houses with timber framing filled in by wattle and daub (woven twigs or branches plastered over with clay or mud mixed with straw). To make these houses more durable, colonists eventually began to cover the outer walls with clapboards, short planks of wood. Clapboard-sided houses were little known in England, where there was a shortage of timber, but became a distinctive feature of American architecture, especially in New England. Until around 1670 roofs were usually covered with thatch or sod, but after that wooden shingles or clay tiles came to be preferred.

Dutch houses in New Amsterdam were typically tall and narrow, like those in the Netherlands, and often built of brick or stone. Philadelphia, unlike most other colonial English cities, also had many brick houses. After a hurricane in 1713 devastated much of the city of Charleston, South Carolina, its residents rebuilt the city using brick.

In Rhode Island, where stone was plentiful, the chimney ends of houses were often built of stone, even if the rest was wood. After disastrous fires that destroyed many of the original wooden houses,

Longhouses and Wigwams ❧

In the area around the northeastern British colonies and in southeastern Canada, there were two main groups of Native Americans, one speaking Algonquian languages and the other Iroquois. The tribes in each group not only spoke closely related languages but also shared many cultural traits, including the way they built their houses.

The main Iroquois tribes made up a confederacy known as the Five Nations (which became the Six Nations in 1720 when an additional tribe joined them). Their name for themselves was Haudenosaunee, "The People of the Longhouse." As a Haudenosaunee diplomat told a group of officials in Quebec in 1653, "We, the five Iroquois nations, compose but one longhouse . . . ; and we have, from time immemorial, dwelt under one and the same roof."

This image reflected the people's traditional dwelling, the longhouse. A typical longhouse was at least 100 feet (30 meters) in length and about 25 to 30 feet (7.5 to 9 meters) wide. It was built of a wooden framework covered with bark or strips of wood, with a curving roof. Several related families lived together in the longhouse, each with their own hearthfire and alcove for sleeping and storage.

Most Algonquian peoples lived in wigwams, with each family having its own dwelling. Some wigwams looked like miniature longhouses, rectangular with curved roofs. Others were more dome shaped. A French soldier named Jolicoeur Charles Bonin wrote this description of a typical Algonquian village and its wigwams (which he calls cabins) during the time of the French and Indian War:

> It is a group of cabins of various shapes and sizes. Some are long as a shed. They are all built and covered with tree bark, with the exception of a strip in the roof about two feet long, to let out the smoke from a fire of the same size. On each side of a cabin, there are beds made of bark spread on sticks and raised seven or eight inches [18 or 20 centimeters] above the ground. The exterior of these cabins is sometimes covered with a mixture of earth and brush to keep out the wind. The doors are likewise of bark hung from the top like blinds, or fastened on one side with wooden withes, making a swinging door.

both Quebec City and Montreal passed regulations requiring all new dwellings to be made of stone. Quebec City also ordered buildings to be semi-detached and two stories tall, with steeply sloped roofs.

Spanish houses in St. Augustine were usually built either of stone or of a kind of concrete made from ground oyster shells, and were roofed with wooden shingles. In the southwest, however, Spanish ranchers and missionaries adapted native building styles and constructed adobe houses with clay-tile roofs. For the wealthy, these houses could be two stories tall, with balconies, covered porches, and a large central courtyard.

The most famous kind of American house was actually introduced by Swedish and Finnish settlers. These Scandinavian colonists came from a heavily forested part of Europe and were experts at handling an axe. (Many English colonists were not, but they soon learned from their Scandinavian neighbors.) It was said that one Swede with an axe and a wooden wedge could cut down twelve huge oaks in a single day. Once the tree trunks were split or roughly squared off, the Swede had nearly all the materials he needed to build a small square house in the style of his homeland. Since all he had to do was notch the ends of the logs and lay them on top of one another, he did not even need nails—which could be expensive and hard to come by in the colonies (tough wooden pegs were often used instead). He and his family could make the house perfectly snug by filling any cracks between the logs with mud, moss, or other natural materials.

Many other settlers, especially the Germans in Pennsylvania, saw the advantages of this Scandinavian building technique and adopted it for their own. It became a favorite, even standard, type of frontier home, taken ever farther west by generations of pioneers. Today we know it as the log cabin.

Additions and Outbuildings

Early colonial houses (and, later, the houses of the poor) were quite small. They had only one or two rooms, where the entire family crowded together to eat, sleep, work, pray, and, occasionally, relax. As colonists became settled and better off, they naturally craved more space. Some built new, larger houses; others simply added on to the house they had.

One of the easiest additions to build was a loft over the main room. Reached by a ladder or a steep flight of narrow stairs, the loft could be used both for storage and as sleeping space, usually for children or servants. Another easy addition was a lean-to built onto the back of the house. The lean-to made a good storage area, and often it also served as a kitchen.

Sometimes it was easiest or made most sense for a family to construct additional buildings near the house. Farms and plantations generally included a number of outbuildings to provide for livestock and various agricultural needs. There could be a henhouse, a stable for horses, a barn for cows, perhaps another barn for storing grains and hay, a toolshed, and a smokehouse (where meat was smoked to preserve it). There might be buildings where certain jobs were done: a brewhouse where the farmwife made beer or ale, a dairy where butter and cheese were made and stored, a cider mill where apples were pressed to make cider. People often had a spring-house, a small building built over a spring, where perishable foods could be kept cool. A family wealthy enough to own a coach or carriage would also have a coach house to keep it in.

A museum houses this collection of furnishings and metal tools used by colonists. The object on the ground in the center of the fireplace is a roasting kitchen, a metal box in which meat could be roasted by the fire.

By the end of the colonial period many southern homes had a separate kitchen building so that the heat from cooking would not make the house hotter, particularly in the summer. On some Virginia plantations, the children of the family slept in outbuildings away from their parents, who slept in the main house. Tobacco plantations had sheds where the tobacco was dried and cured.

On these plantations and on other farms that used slave labor, there might also be workshops where slaves did spinning and other tasks. And there were slave quarters—often tiny, drafty, leaking cabins with dirt floors. On small farms, slaves might not even have houses but would sleep in a barn or tobacco shed. When possible, slaves and free African Americans built houses with some African features, such as a square central room and roof thatch made from palmetto leaves.

Light and Heat

By modern standards, colonial homes were rather dark and gloomy. Windows were generally few and small, and glass was rare and expensive in the colonies, especially before the 1700s. To let in light, window openings were typically covered with oiled paper, waxed cloth, or thin slices of animal horn. Windows had wooden shutters that could be closed to keep out cold drafts, but the closed shutters kept out light, too. On nice days, however, the door could be left open, which let both light and fresh air into the house. Dutch settlers built their doors in two sections so that they could open the top and leave the bottom shut. Colonial doorways in general were rather low, so that most adults had to stoop when they entered a house.

There were only a few artificial light sources. Beeswax candles were the best, as they burned cleanly, but they were expensive. Tallow candles were lower quality and made more smoke, but a housewife could make them from animal fat left over from butchering and cooking. Another source of candle wax was the bayberry bush, native to North America and especially common in New England. When its berries were boiled in water, they released a waxy substance that could be skimmed out, remelted, and poured into candle molds. Bayberry candles also had a very pleasant fragrance, especially just after they went out. Some colonists would light bayberry candles and then extinguish them right before visitors arrived, to give the home a welcoming smell.

If candles were not available, colonists had a couple of other options. One was the rushlight, commonly used back in Europe. This was just a length of dried reed soaked in grease; held in place by a metal clamp, it gave off a smoky, smelly, feeble light. The other main choice was candlewood, a type of pitch-filled "fat" or pine. It was cut

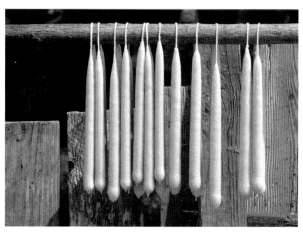

Candles could be made by pouring melted tallow or beeswax into molds or by dipping wicks into melted wax over and over until the candles reached the desired thickness. These hand-dipped beeswax candles were made at a living history museum as part of a demonstration of colonial crafts.

A colonial hall or kitchen was the setting of many daily activities. Here, children play and a grandfather peels apples, while women work at baking, cooking, churning butter, and spinning.

into roughly candle-sized pieces, which burned like small torches. Colonists in New England, New York, and Virginia all used candlewood, as did many of the native peoples.

The other source of added light was simply the fire in the fireplace. Colonial fireplaces were quite large, as much as 10 feet (3 meters) wide. In northern colonies, they were often placed in the center of the house so that their heat would be more evenly distributed through the home—although some houses were so drafty that only someone right next to the fire would be warmed by it. German colonists introduced woodburning stoves, which were more efficient heat sources. One of Benjamin Franklin's notable inventions was an improved version of such stoves, which he called the "Pennsylvania Fire Place" but we know as the Franklin stove.

In most of the Spanish colonies, heating was needed far less than in other parts of North America. Often a charcoal brazier was enough to produce extra warmth when it was wanted, although this did not produce much light.

Furniture

Many colonists arrived in North America with little or no furniture except the wooden chests in which they packed whatever clothing and household goods they had brought along. The chests— often beautifully carved in the case of wealthy people—were long used for both storage and seating in colonial homes.

Clothing and other household items were stored in chests such as this one, which was made in Connecticut between 1650 and 1680. Wooden chests also provided extra seating when needed.

For early settlers and poor people, the only other seating might be short upended logs, known as "block cheers." Gradually, colonists made or acquired stools and benches. A bench with a high back was called a settle, and its design protected those seated on it from drafts.

Before the 1700s, chairs were not very common; many families had just one, reserved for the father or an honored guest. Most chairs were hard wood or wood with woven rush seats, although they might be softened with cushions. Upholstered chairs did not become popular for some time, and then only the well-to-do could afford them.

For much of the colonial period, a family's table was usually just a board (or two boards nailed together) laid across supports. Sometimes the lid of a wooden packing case was used as a tabletop. One advantage of this kind of table was that it could be taken down and leaned against a wall if more space was needed. The table and seating were in the house's main (or only) room, called the hall, and many other activities besides eating took place here. Generally this was where a housewife did much of her work, so the room would contain her spinning wheel, baskets of wool and flax, a butter churn, cooking utensils, washtubs, and possibly a weaving loom. There would be barrels of stored grain, and hanging from the ceiling beams might be

Outdoor ovens such as this one at the Charles Towne Landing historic site made it possible to bake without heating up the whole house—an important consideration in the hot and humid South. This could also have served as a community oven, used by people who did not have their own ovens.

slabs of bacon, dried fruits and vegetables, and bunches of herbs. Clothes and tools hung from pegs on the walls. Possibly there would be a cupboard or cabinet for storing dishes, spoons, and napkins.

At night the hall became a bedroom. For some time, though, bedrolls were much more common than beds. In New England, the mother and father of a family sometimes had a "turn-up bedstead." This was a bed attached to the wall with hinges. During the day it could be folded up against the wall, out of the way. Like most colonial beds, it had a sturdy wooden frame and ropes tightly crisscrossed to support the mattress.

Mattresses were stuffed with corn husks, straw, rags, bits of wool—whatever suitable material people could get. Some colonists—particularly the Dutch in New York—had the luxury of feather-stuffed mattresses and quilts. Dutch and German colonists also had a tradition of building the main bed into an alcove in the wall, which made it very cozy. English and French settlers preferred a bed with heavy wool curtains hanging around it to keep in heat. Usually only the parents had a bed like this (if they could afford it); in a house with more than one room, this bed would be the main piece of furniture in a room next to the hall. A trundle bed, for young children, might pull out from under it.

Gardens

A very important part of most colonial homesteads was the garden. In the 1700s formal gardens—with ornamental plants, carefully trimmed hedges, fountains and statues, and lovely pathways—became fashionable among the wealthy. Some plantations, for example, had many acres devoted to such gardens. But for the average family, gardens were more valued for their usefulness than their beauty.

Most gardens were just outside the house, as close to the kitchen as possible. Often the well that supplied all the family's water for drinking, cooking, and washing was located here, too. Tending the garden was mainly the housewife's responsibility. She raised vegetables such as carrots, onions, turnips, peas, radishes, beans, lettuce, cabbage, asparagus, cucumbers, pumpkins, and, in the Spanish colonies, tomatoes and peppers.

Colonial housewives grew many herbs, including parsley, sage, savory, thyme, spearmint, dill, feverfew, angelica, fennel, and lavender. Many herbs were for cooking, but many were for making medicines, and some were for both. There were few doctors in the colonies, especially early on and in rural areas, so many women tended their families and neighbors in times of illness. Some houses even had a stillroom near the kitchen, where the housewife could make and store her herbal remedies.

Vegetable gardens such as this one at Mount Vernon, George Washington's Virginia estate, provided much of a family's food. Young plants had to be carefully tended throughout the spring.

Flowers were grown, too, for beauty, fragrance, and usefulness—some were edible, some were medicinal, and some could be used to make dyes for cloth. Among the flowers grown by colonists were roses, marigolds, hollyhocks, pansies, carnations, lilies, tulips, and daffodils. Many fruits could be gathered in the wild, or were grown in orchards, but sometimes kitchen gardens had melons, strawberries, apples, pears, and peaches. Gardens in St. Augustine might include orange trees, originally imported from Spain—the beginning of Florida's citrus industry.

Seventeenth–century settlers in the colony of New Sweden
dressed in the styles of their northern homelands.

CHAPTER FIVE

Clothing and Personal Well-Being

WHEN COLONISTS WERE FIRST ESTABLISHING THEM-
selves in North America, simple survival was their main concern. Even the wealthy had little time or energy to worry about fashion or other aspects of their appearance. Clothing tended to be simpler and more practical than in Europe. It had to be hard wearing, too, because it was difficult to replace. In the early years, very little cloth was available for sale in the colonies, and what was available was expensive. Later, as colonial cities and trade began to thrive, cloth became more abundant and affordable. By the early 1700s, middle- and upper-class colonists were able to dress more elaborately and fashionably.

Cloth Production

Throughout the colonial period, many women—assisted by their daughters and sometimes sons—made all or at least part of their family's wardrobe. Producing cloth and clothing was a major part of their daily lives.

The process started with preparing wool or flax, the two most commonly used fibers, for spinning. To remove dirt and straighten the fibers, wool had to be carded and flax combed. Flax was made into thread using a small spinning wheel turned by a foot pedal. For wool, the spinner used a large "walking wheel" that she turned by hand, walking back and forth as she drew out the fibers. A good spinner could produce six skeins, or coils, of wool yarn in a day; in the process she would walk more than a dozen miles (19 kilometers).

After spinning, the fibers were wound into skeins, and both wool and flax thread were washed. The flax was then bleached with ashes and hot water, buttermilk, or a solution of powdered limestone. Wool thread or yarn was sometimes dyed at this stage, but sometimes the wool had been dyed before spinning (in which case it was "dyed in the wool"—the origin of this phrase). All dyes came from natural substances: wild or garden flowers and herbs, berries, bark, nut shells and husks, or even clay. Many southern plantations grew indigo, which supplied a favorite blue dye, and some of it was sold by indigo peddlers who traveled throughout the colonies.

Wool yarn was now ready for knitting into stockings, caps, and mittens. Children, especially girls, learned to knit as young as age four and became very skilled and efficient. Most of the flax and wool, though, was used for weaving. Many women wove their own cloth, but those who did not own a loom would take their spun thread to the local weaver, usually a man.

Male or female, colonial weavers made several different kinds of cloth. Linen was woven from pure flax. Linsey-woolsey was a mix of flax and wool. There were also different kinds of woolen cloth, such as flannel and broadcloth. During the 1700s southern plantations started growing more cotton, so there was cloth made of part cotton and part wool or linen. Toward the end of the century, all-cotton cloth was common in the south, especially for slaves' clothes. Some southern colonies also experimented with producing silk.

Once a housewife had cloth, she would bleach it (again) if it was linen and dye it (if it was not already dyed) if it was wool. Then she could finally start making clothing. Linen was used for shirts, caps, kerchiefs, and undergarments, as well as for sheets, tablecloths, and

One of the first steps in making clothes was spinning thread or yarn, a chore that colonial women spent many, many hours doing.

handkerchiefs. Almost everything else was made out of the wool or mixed-fiber fabrics. Much of the sewing would be done during winter.

In general the whole process of making a piece of clothing, from preparing the fibers to sewing the final seam, could take weeks or months (or more than a year in the case of linen, because the flax required many more stages of treatment). In an emergency, though, a woolen garment could be produced in a week or less.

This Pilgrim couple is depicted in their Sunday best, as imagined by nineteenth-century artist Howard Pyle.

What People Wore

English colonists were surprised to find that North American winters were much colder than what they were used to, and summers were much warmer. Nevertheless, they usually continued to dress the same way as they had in the mother country, although they might add more layers in the winter. (People were used to dressing in several layers in any case.) French settlers in Canada, on the other hand, had such severe winters to contend with and so much trouble raising sheep that they often switched to wearing garments of leather and fur in styles similar to what the native peoples wore.

For both women and men, the first layer was a shirt and stockings. Women's shirts, though, were much longer, reaching to the ankle. Sometimes they were referred to as shifts or chemises. They frequently had a drawstring neckline so that they could be pulled down to breastfeed a baby. Over her shift, a woman often put on stays, a cloth undergarment that incorporated strips of metal, whalebone, or other material to stiffen it; it went around her waist. Next she might put on one or more petticoats or underskirts. Then she tied on a pocket, which at the time was a flat rectangular bag that she could reach through a slit in her skirt. The skirt was the next layer, followed by the bodice, a kind of fitted blouse, which usually had detachable sleeves that were tied on at the shoulders. The average woman would finish her outfit with a linen cap on her head and a kerchief around her neck. Usually she also wore a linen apron, but she would put on a wool apron when she was cooking because wool was less flammable—there was always the danger of sparks landing on her when she worked near the fire.

After his shirt and stockings, a man would put on breeches, pants that ended a little below the knee. Next he donned a waistcoat, or vest. Over that he would wear a jacket, unless he was doing manual labor that made it inappropriate. (Backcountry men, though, dressed in a much different style, typically wearing full-length trousers and, very often, leather or deerskin shirts or jackets.) For some kinds of work, a man put on an apron to protect his clothes—blacksmiths, for example, wore leather aprons. The average man usually also wore a cap on his head and a kerchief around his neck.

Attended by an African servant, this couple on a plantation in the West Indies in the 1700s wears light colors, fairly simple styles, and broad-brimmed hats as protection against the heat and sun.

A man's footwear would generally be either boots or moccasins. Women, too, often wore moccasins. It was an article of Indian clothing that many colonists found very practical. Moccasins were fairly easy to make and repair, they could be stuffed with moss or wool or other materials to make them warmer, and even though they were not waterproof, they dried quickly near a fire. For outerwear in cold or rainy weather, both women and men usually wore woolen cloaks.

This illustration contrasts two different styles of seventeenth-century clothing. On the left, a Puritan couple dresses plainly and modestly, while the well-to-do English settlers on the right dress in an elaborate style that shows off their wealth and love of fashion.

For Sundays and special occasions, colonists typically exchanged these workaday clothes for their best outfits. The garments were similar in style, but the best clothes might include fine linen collars, shoes with metal buckles, some lace trim, and other flourishes. The fabrics would be better quality, often dyed black, which was a special color because it was difficult to produce with the available dyes. The pictures that we see of the Pilgrims and Puritans in their dark clothing with their tall hats and big white collars portray these colonists in their Sunday best. At other times they, like most people of the time, wore rich, bright colors: reds, russets, blues, greens, and yellows.

Puritan authorities did, however, frown on people displaying too much pride or vanity in the way they dressed. At various times, New England colonies passed laws restricting how much lace or silk or ribbon or fancy buttons people (especially the common people) could wear. These laws were frequently broken, even though the punishment might be a sizable fine. The Quakers and some German religious groups encouraged an even plainer, extremely modest style of dress, similar to what many Amish people still wear today.

At the opposite extreme, wealthy people in cities and on plantations, especially in the 1700s, wore very expensive, elaborate clothing. The fabric was often imported, sometimes from India and China, and could be richly patterned in many colors. Accessories included silk stockings (held up with ribbon garters), elegant shoes, velvet headdresses, and hoops to hold out women's skirts.

As for children, from the time they left swaddling, they were generally dressed like miniature adults, except that young boys and girls both wore long gowns. Boys started wearing pants like their fathers' around age six or seven. Among English colonists, this event was known as "being breeched," and it was often an occasion for a celebration with friends and family.

A well-dressed gentleman around the time of the American Revolution. He is wearing buckled shoes, stockings, knee breeches, a ruffle-sleeved shirt, a waistcoat, a long coat with brass buttons, and a tricorn hat.

Laundry

The Pilgrims reached the New World on a Saturday and devoted the next day to worship and prayer on board the *Mayflower*. They had been on the ship for two months, and during the voyage it had not been possible to wash clothes. On Monday the women came ashore, found a pond, and set about doing laundry. This established a New England tradition that lasted for generations: Monday was wash day.

Often, though, laundry was done only one Monday a month—or even one day a season. This was mainly because washing clothes was such hard work. First, most housewives had to make their own soap, a smelly, dirty, day-long job. They used grease and fat, saved from cooking and butchering, and lye, which was derived from a mixture of ashes and water. These ingredients were put into a cauldron over a fire outdoors and boiled together. The mixture had to be stirred constantly (a task often given to girls), and the result was a soft, jelly-like soap.

On wash day water had to be hauled and heated to fill the washtubs, or the laundry had to be hauled to the nearest creek or other water source (hopefully this was not much farther away than the kitchen garden). The soap was rubbed into the clothes, which were scrubbed against a washboard or rock. Then they had to be rinsed repeatedly to get all the dirt and soap out. After the women wrung out as much water as possible, they laid out or hung up the clothes to dry in the sun and wind—a process that could take days, since many of the fabrics were thick and heavy. Some of the heaviest garments, especially the outer layers of people's outfits, were never laundered but were just brushed clean now and then.

Cleanliness and Grooming

As hard as it was to wash clothes, it was nearly as difficult for colonists to keep themselves clean. Most tried to at least wash their faces once a day, and their hands before they ate. But washing the whole body was a rare event. Probably hair washing was, too. In general, hair care was limited to daily combing or brushing. Girls and women in the backcountry sometimes conditioned their hair with bear grease, as did Native American women.

As far as hairstyles went, during the earlier part of the colonial period, both women and men were most interested in simply keeping their hair out of the way while they worked. In any case, they usually had their heads covered for warmth or modesty or both. Men tended to wear their hair short or collar length till about the mid-1600s, when longer hair came into favor. Farmers, craftsmen, and laborers would keep hair out of the way by braiding it or tying it back with a cord or ribbon, but gentlemen might wear theirs in long waves or curls. Toward the end of the century, upper-class men started cutting their hair very short, or even shaving their heads, and wore powdered wigs—a fashion that lasted for another hundred years or so.

This portrait of Boston clergyman Cotton Mather, around 1710, shows him wearing a powdered wig.

Fashionable women in the 1700s wore increasingly elaborate hairstyles, with their hair teased and piled high and puffed higher still with the addition of straw, horsehair, wool, or other materials. After spending many hours with a hairdresser to achieve such a style, a woman tried to preserve it as long as possible. So she would not brush out her hair, and as a result would be far more troubled by lice and fleas than were women who styled their hair more simply.

Insects were a great nuisance in colonial times—lice, fleas, bedbugs, mosquitoes, and flies in particular. Sometimes they were more than a nuisance. Mosquitoes might carry malaria, while lice could carry typhus, a potentially deadly disease that spread easily in crowded conditions, such as those aboard ship.

Another disease common both aboard ship and among early colonists was scurvy, caused by lack of vitamin C. Among the effects of scurvy were bleeding gums, loosening teeth, and foul breath. Even without scurvy, dental health was poor, especially as many colonists had a taste for sweets. If they wanted to clean their teeth, the most they could generally do was wipe them with a bit of cloth; there were no toothbrushes.

There were also no bathrooms. Very few people even had chamber pots until around 1700. Instead they used an outdoor privy, no matter what the time of day or night or what the weather. On a dark winter night, going to the outhouse must have been something of an ordeal for a healthy adult, not to mention a young child or a sick person.

The Influence of Native Clothing ❧

Europeans were used to dressing in layers—often elaborate layers—of clothing, so colonists were often shocked by what Native Americans wore. Men might wear no more than a breechclout (a sort of knee-length loincloth) and leggings. Women often wore just a skirt, or a simple sleeveless dress made of animal skin. Except in bad weather, young children usually wore nothing at all. Most Europeans found these ways of dressing immodest, barbaric, and even sinful, so they adopted very little native clothing—among the English in general, only moccasins. Some men, though, particularly in the backcountry, found Indian-style leggings of leather or heavy cloth very useful for protecting their lower legs from thorns, underbrush, snakes, and the like.

French trappers, who spent most of their time in the wilderness, adopted not only moccasins and leggings but also native-style shirts or coats made from the skins of deer, moose, caribou, or bear. They were also quick to make use of snowshoes, which had been perfected by the native peoples of Canada and the northeast. Otherwise it would have been almost impossible to get around on foot during the winter. In another example of subarctic conditions inspiring Europeans to follow native ways of dress, period illustrations of fishermen in Newfoundland show some of them wearing hooded parkas, probably made of fur or animal skin, similar to traditional Inuit garb.

In some ways, colonists had more influence on native clothing than the other way around. Traders often paid Indian hunters and trappers for furs with blankets and bolts of cloth. A blanket or length of cloth draped rather like a toga became a common outer garment for both men and women in Canada and the northeast. Among the Iroquois and some other tribes, both sexes also came to like European-style linen shirts, especially with ruffles. And many native women became fond of imported blue or red cloth for their skirts.

Mohawk chief Thayendanegea (Joseph Brant) is wearing a combination of European and Native American clothing in this portrait painted around the time of the American Revolution.

Fishermen in Newfoundland, Canada, prepare their codfish catch for drying, salting, and shipping. The Canadian fishing industry was big business, and the fish were sold in both the colonies and Europe.

CHAPTER SIX ᘓ
Food and Drink

IN THEIR HOMELANDS, MANY OF THE

Europeans who came to North America had been living in towns, working as craftspeople, shopkeepers, and laborers. In the colonies, most of them became farmers. For some, this was why they had come to the New World: they wanted to own land and to support their families on it. In the early decades of the colonies, too, there was little opportunity to practice their former trades. It took time for towns to develop and for food production to reach a level at which some people in the community could be spared for other work. One of the greatest challenges early colonists and pioneers faced was getting enough food—and making sure it lasted through the winter.

Getting and Preserving Food

Grain was a major part of every colonist's diet, and it was the main crop raised on most farms. Settlers had some difficulty at first with producing European grains—wheat, barley, rye, and oats—and found it much easier to grow the native staple, maize. English colonists called maize "Indian corn," since "corn" was their word for "grain," and most Americans continue to refer to maize as "corn." After a few years in the New World, colonists learned how to grow European grains in American soil (although wheat still did not grow well in many northern areas), but they continued to grow maize as well. With the maize they might also grow squash and beans, all planted together in the native style, and they might plant some of their fields with peas or lentils, which were additional staples. Other vegetables were grown in the household garden. Many farmers also planted orchards of fruit trees, especially apples.

All of the colonists' farm animals initially had to be brought from Europe. The early settlers could bring only small livestock: chickens, goats, and sheep. It was some years before the Pilgrims, for example, could import horses and cattle. They bred these animals so successfully, though, that in the 1630s they grew prosperous from selling livestock to the new colony of Massachusetts Bay.

Farmers used horses and oxen to pull their carts and plows. Cows and goats were milked. Chickens provided eggs in warm weather and meat the rest of the year (chickens that lay eggs year-round are a modern development). The colonists raised sheep mainly for their wool, which made them too valuable to eat except in an emergency. (They could also be milked, but most North American colonists seem not to have liked sheep's milk very much.) Cattle were probably only slaughtered for meat and leather once they could no longer pull a plow or give milk. The animal most commonly raised for meat was the pig, which required little care and would eat almost anything. Some colonists also kept geese, but mostly for their feathers, which could be gathered without harming the animal, rather than for their meat.

The North American environment provided a bounty of other food sources—although at first many colonists were not able to take advantage of them. For instance, fish were plentiful in Plymouth Bay, but none of the Pilgrims knew how to catch them or had the appropriate gear for doing so. Eventually, though, the coastal colonies had many skilled fishermen. Fish were also plentiful in the continent's creeks, lakes, and rivers. There was plenty of shellfish, too, such as clams and mussels, that could be dug up or gathered on many shores.

In the forests there were deer, moose, and wild turkeys. Settlers living in what is now Canada also ate the meat of caribou, porcupine, and beaver, and many colonists ate squirrel, raccoon, and bear meat.

All kinds of game birds could be found in marshes and meadows, including ducks, wild geese, and pigeons. Again, it took some time for the colonists to take full advantage of these resources, because many of them first had to acquire guns and learn how to use them—back in Europe, only gentlemen had been allowed to own weapons.

The environment also provided numerous wild plant foods, especially berries, nuts, and herbs. From Native Americans, northern colonists learned how to tap maple trees for their sap and make syrup, which became a favorite sweetener. After English and Dutch settlers imported honeybees, the colonies also had honey. Sugar and molasses were available, too, but could be rather expensive since they were imported from the West Indies. Other imported foods that could be purchased by well-off colonists were spices (such as pepper, cinnamon, cloves, and ginger), raisins, currants, and olives. The Spanish in Florida grew their own citrus fruits, but colonists farther north had to import them.

Here slaves are cutting sugarcane on a plantation in the West Indies. The crop will be processed into sugar, molasses, and rum.

Some of the foods that farm families preserved for the winter included grain, bacon, and dried fruits, vegetables, and herbs. Along with the bacon, hams were smoked, and so were other kinds of meat. Other ways to make meat last were salting and drying it. Many types of fish could also be smoked, salted, or dried, and some types could be pickled (preserved in vinegar). Peas, beans, and corn were all dried. Radishes, carrots, beets, onions, turnips, and parsnips were stored in root cellars or barrels packed with straw. Numerous vegetables and fruits were preserved by pickling. Housewives also turned fruits into jams and jellies. In Pennsylvania and neighboring areas they boiled apples, pears, lemons, and plums down into fruit "butters." Milk was made into cheese and butter, which kept for many months even without refrigeration.

In the Canadian winter, refrigeration was no problem: It often was so cold that farmers could carry milk to market in sacks, which did not leak because the milk was frozen solid. In Canada colonists could grow nothing from November through April, so they had to be especially careful about preserving enough food and storing it properly. Luckily, the cold helped. Many Canadians had an unheated storehouse for meat, which safely froze there and could be removed and thawed over the fire when it was needed.

Cooking and Eating

In the average family, the wife and daughters did the food preservation and preparation. Wealthy households, though, had servants or slaves to do this work, under the wife's supervision. Nearly all cooking was done in the fireplace in the kitchen or hall. This fireplace was often large enough to have more than one fire burning in it at the same time, enabling the housewife or cook to simultaneously prepare dishes that required different levels of heat.

Often there was a stone or brick oven built into the chimney, but in some villages and towns, women did not have this convenience. They took their bread to a community oven or bakehouse for baking. In a city they might just buy their bread from a bakery. Baking could also be done in a covered bake kettle, sometimes known as a Dutch oven, which was set in the fireplace with hot coals heaped on and around it.

All colonial cookware had legs so that it could be placed directly over the coals. When room for a bigger fire was needed under the pots, they could be hung up by hooks or chains that attached to a horizontal bar fastened within the fireplace. Colonial pots and kettles were made of brass or iron and could weigh as much as 40 pounds (18 kilograms)—cooking, like most other housework and farmwork, required strength. Many families had only one or two pots or kettles in which to do their cooking, but some also had a variety of smaller, lighter cookware such as skillets, griddles, gridirons, toasting forks, and even waffle irons. For roasting meat, there might be a kind of cylindrical metal box called a roasting kitchen, or a spit that had to be kept constantly turning. In many families, this was one of the chores children did. Sometimes, though, a piece of meat was just hung by a string over the fire to roast.

Most colonists ate three meals a day: breakfast, dinner, and supper. Breakfast was eaten before the day's main work began, supper around seven or eight at night. People generally had dinner, the main meal, in the early afternoon. French Canadian farmers, though, made breakfast and supper their most solid meals, and had a light dinner and another light meal in late afternoon. And backcountry settlers typically ate just two meals a day, one in the morning and one in mid-afternoon.

A Busy Girl ✎

Abigail Foote grew up on a farm in Connecticut. In this diary entry from 1775, when she was about fifteen years old, she lists the work and other activities she did in a single day.

Fix'd gown for Prude,—Mend Mother's Riding-hood,—Spun short thread,—Fix'd two gowns for Welsh's girls,—Carded tow,—Spun linen,—Worked on Cheese-basket,—Hatchel'd flax with Hannah, we did 51 lbs. apiece,—Pleated and ironed,—Read a Sermon of Dodridge's,—Spooled a piece,—Milked the cows,—Spun linen, did 50 knots,—Made a broom of Guinea wheat straw,—Spun thread to whiten,—Set a Red dye,—Had two Scholars from Mrs. Taylor's,—I carded two pounds of whole wool and felt Nationly,—Spun harness twine,—Scoured the pewter.

Barrels of rum were shipped from the West Indies to colonies farther north as well as to Europe.

During the busiest parts of the agricultural year, farmers often did not stop to come back to the house for dinner but ate something quick and easy out in the fields. For most meals, however, the average family ate together at their table. Sometimes the housewife just set a pot of food in the middle of the table, and everyone ate directly out of it. Another common way of serving was to set the food out on round pewter platters called chargers, and then dish it up onto individual plates. Very often, especially in the seventeenth century, each plate was shared by two people.

Plates were typically made of wood and were called trenchers, although well-off families might have pewter plates. In the 1700s, china began to come into use among wealthy colonists. At this time, too, forks became a common eating utensil in the middle and upper classes. Earlier, most people, however rich or poor, ate with spoons (made of wood, pewter, horn, or silver) and their fingers. They also had knives for cutting up meat, but these were often the same knives they carried with them throughout the day to use in their work.

Colonists generally drank from tankards, mugs, cups, or bowls made of wood, leather, pottery, pewter, horn, dried gourds, or silver; drinking glasses were rare during much of the 1600s. It was also rare for each person to have their own cup or mug to drink from. Instead, there would be one or two beverage containers on the table, which would be passed around from person to person.

Drinks

One of the Pilgrims' greatest surprises in the New World was the water: It was drinkable. In Europe most water sources, especially in cities, were so polluted that the water was unsafe. People's everyday drinks had been ale, beer, or wine. But the colonists soon ran out of the stores of these beverages that they brought with them, and it was a while before they were able to make or purchase more. So they had to drink water—and they found that they liked it.

This silver teapot was made by Paul Revere. In the 1700s silver tea services were highly prized by wealthy families in the British colonies.

As soon as they were able, though, colonists did supply themselves with other beverages. A favorite in New England was apple cider. Pear cider, called perry, was another popular drink. Many northern colonists drank a great deal of milk. Well-off people could drink imported coffee, tea, and hot chocolate, all of which began to be available in the late 1600s. The wealthy also enjoyed a variety of imported wines. The French and Spanish planted vineyards in their colonies, so settlers there had some local wines.

Although the Puritans and Quakers both disapproved of drunkenness (as they disapproved of other kinds of excess and overindulgence), alcoholic drinks were abundant in the British colonies. As in Europe, such beverages were often drunk throughout the day, even at breakfast and even by children—usually watered down, though. Much of the cider that New Englanders enjoyed was hard cider. In

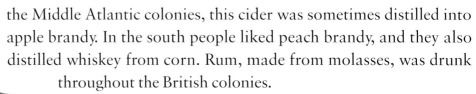

the Middle Atlantic colonies, this cider was sometimes distilled into apple brandy. In the south people liked peach brandy, and they also distilled whiskey from corn. Rum, made from molasses, was drunk throughout the British colonies.

Dutch, German, and English settlers were all very fond of beer, which they brewed from hops and wheat or barley—and sometimes incorporated corn, pumpkins, walnuts, parsnips, or sassafras root (the origin of root beer) when traditional ingredients were not available. French Canadians made a kind of beer from the needles of spruce trees. Among British colonists in particular, a number of mixed drinks were popular, especially flip. This was beer and rum sweetened with molasses, sugar, or even dried pumpkin. It was heated right before serving by thrusting a red-hot poker into it.

This earthenware tea caddy (a jar for storing tea) was made for a Pennsylvania woman named Esther Smith in 1767.

Regional Foodways

Many colonial foodways were continuations of European traditions. Of course, the New World offered new foods, a number of which became important for colonists, especially pumpkin, beans, squash, cranberries, and above all maize, or corn.

Sometimes colonists adapted their old familiar recipes to incorporate these ingredients; sometimes they learned and used native recipes. An example of the first trend was "Indian pudding," cornmeal mixed with milk, butter, and a little molasses or maple sugar—a popular breakfast in many areas. An example of the second was succotash, corn and beans cooked together in fat.

Exactly what foods people in the colonies ate, and how they prepared them, could vary widely from region to region. For example, peppers and tomatoes were common ingredients in Spanish colonial

A Farm Family's Day ✑

Most colonists in North America were farmers or farmworkers—as many as 75 percent at the time of the American Revolution. Much of the agriculture in the south was devoted to raising marketable and exportable products such as tobacco, rice, and indigo. But throughout the colonies, everyone depended on farms for most of what they ate. And many farm families were able to live on just the crops and livestock they raised themselves. To do this, though, everyone in the family had to put in long days of working together.

A New England farm family's day in the 1600s would begin as early as 4:30 A.M.—even though breakfast would not be eaten for another two hours. Livestock had to be fed and cows milked before the people could eat, and there was also time to get a little work done in field or garden. Meanwhile, the mother would be building up the fire and preparing breakfast.

After eating, everyone got down to serious work. Men and older children had plowing or sowing or other tasks to do in the fields; women and younger children had cleaning, cooking, food preserving, gardening, candle and cloth making, and other household chores to do. Around 11, people took a short break, resting and drinking a mug or two of cider. Then it was back to work until around two in the afternoon, which was dinnertime.

After dinner, livestock needed more looking after. There might be more to do in the fields or orchards, too, but if not, this was a good time for a farmer to make and repair tools—or he might even have a chance to do a little hunting or fishing now. The farmwife would be almost done with cooking for the day, since supper would be a simple meal, but she still had plenty of work. If nothing else, there was always spinning.

Suppertime was around 6 P.M. After that, there was finally a little time for relaxation. But no one stayed up much past 8:30, because another long workday lay ahead.

Many colonial families, such as these New England farmers in the 1600s, let their chickens and ducks range freely in the farmyard. The birds provided eggs in warm weather and meat for the pot the rest of the year.

cooking but were not used elsewhere. Most English, Dutch, and German colonists disliked potatoes, but they were a staple for Scots-Irish colonists who began settling the backcountry in the 1700s. Rice was very popular in the south—it was successfully raised on plantations in the Carolinas thanks to the expertise of slaves who had cultivated rice in Africa—but it does not seem to have been eaten much at all in the north during this period.

Religion could have a strong effect on people's eating habits. Both Puritans and Quakers believed that food should be plain and simple—not highly spiced or elaborately served. They discouraged feasting and overindulgence. Catholic and Anglican colonists, on the other hand, had many religious holidays for which feasting was part of the traditional celebrations. Catholics also had a number of days in the year, including all Fridays and Lent (the forty days before Easter), when they were supposed to fast by not eating meat. This made fish even more important to them as a protein source.

Different groups of British colonists tended to have different favorite foods and cooking methods. New Englanders liked to bake much of their food, often in the form of pies. From the Indians they learned to slow-bake beans in an earthenware pot, the origin of the dish known today as Boston baked beans. This was often accompanied by a bread they called "rye 'n' injun," made from a mixture of rye flour and cornmeal. The crust was so hard that they used it as a spoon to eat the beans. Another distinctive New England dish was the boiled dinner, which was just plain meat and vegetables boiled together, without seasonings, in a pot of water.

Virginia colonists were fond of simmering or frying their food. Fried chicken became a favorite early on. Another popular dish was the fricassee, which was made of two or three kinds of meat simmered together with a variety of herbs; sometimes eggs, wine, and oysters were added.

For poor people and slaves in the south, the common foods were "cornmeal mush" (grits), leafy greens (often cooked with pork fat), and ham or bacon. Whenever possible, slaves also added foods that were familiar to them from Africa; these included black-eyed peas, yams, and okra.

The cooking in the Middle Atlantic colonies was influenced by British, Dutch, and German traditions. Apple dumplings, cream cheese, and fruit butters were specialties of the English Quakers. Germans contributed sauerkraut, various kinds of sausage, and scrapple (fried cakes made from meat scraps cooked with cornmeal). The Dutch introduced coleslaw, cookies, waffles, and crullers (deep-fried twists of sweetened dough).

One food that we generally associate with either Manhattan or New England was actually borrowed from the French Canadians. Their *chaudière*—a soup or stew of salted codfish, potatoes, onions, and milk—was adapted in the English-speaking colonies, where it became much loved as chowder.

Everyone was expected to attend Sunday worship in Plymouth Colony.

CHAPTER SEVEN ❧
Leisure Time

MOST COLONIAL PEOPLE HAD TO WORK VERY

hard. Opportunities for recreation were few and precious. Even for many of those who observed Sunday as a day of rest, there was still some farmwork and housework that would have to be done. And for the Puritans, just because it was a day of rest did not mean it was a time to relax—they had both a morning and an afternoon church service, and people were expected to spend the rest of the day in prayer and Bible study.

Puritans strongly disapproved of many recreations because they believed they were a waste of time. The Quakers also had strict views on how people should spend their leisure time (if they had any) and favored useful activities, such as gardening. As a result, Pennsylvania became renowned for having many of the most beautiful gardens and knowledgeable botanists in North America.

Mixing Work and Play

Colonists were often able to make a virtue of necessity and turn work into a fun-filled social occasion. They observed the Native Americans around them doing this after their corn harvest, when everyone joined together to husk the corn. Colonists adapted the custom and came up with the husking bee. The neighbors who gathered to husk the corn helped one another get through what could be a tedious chore by exchanging stories, gossip, jokes, news, and opinions while they did it. This was also an opportunity for unmarried men and women to spend time together. In some places, if a young man happened to husk an ear of red corn, he was allowed to give a kiss to the girl of his choice. Often a husking bee ended with a shared meal or with drinking and dancing.

Colonial women developed other kinds of work bees, such as sewing bees. At a quilting bee everyone joined in to help a woman finish a quilt that she had pieced together from scraps of worn-out clothing. At the next gathering they would help another member of the group. Women also got together to knit and to spin. Some spinning parties might be held outdoors, on a village green, for example. They could be quite large, drawing women from miles around, who rode to the party on horseback, each with her flax wheel tied onto the saddle behind her.

Men also had work parties, especially to help their neighbors cut firewood, clear a field (such gatherings were called "log rollings" and "stump-pulling frolics"), or raise a new house or barn. These events were especially common among Swedish, German, and Quaker settlers. While the men raised a barn or pulled the stumps from a field, the women often joined together to prepare a feast that everyone shared when the work was done.

Pennsylvania Germans made a similar festive occasion out of the autumn hog butchering. It began before dawn on a November morning, and the whole community worked all day cutting up meat, making sausage and scrapple, and smoking hams over hickory-wood fires. At the end everyone shared some rye whiskey, and then each family went home, taking a portion of meat with them.

Sports and Games

Nearly all colonists enjoyed at least some sports and games. Quakers frowned on most of these recreations, but they did believe in the benefits of exercise and encouraged people to swim in the summer and ice skate in the winter. Ice skating was also a favorite winter activity among Dutch and Puritan colonists. Although Puritans opposed a number of sports and amusements, they felt that "outward recreation" was useful and even necessary for good health, so long as people did not get over-enthusiastic about it or neglect their religious duties in order to pursue it. Officials in Massachusetts organized formal athletic exercises and competitions as part of militia training, and at Harvard College students were supposed to have a period of physical activity each day.

Bowls, or lawn bowling, was a popular outdoor game in both the Dutch and English colonies.

The Puritans were serious about their sports. They were not to be played on Sundays, but when they were played, it was important that there be well-understood rules for everyone to follow. In England there had been a rowdy ball game that was often played by entire villages, half the people at one end of the main street, half at the other. Each team tried to get the ball to the opposite end of the village and stop the other team from doing the same—by whatever means possible. The Puritans took this sport and imposed rules and order on it. Their version was soon known as the "Boston game"; today it is American football. The sport referred to as the "Massachusetts game" or "New England game" was an adaptation of English games played with a bat and ball; it was one of the immediate forerunners of baseball.

Such team sports were less popular in the south. There, one of the most popular sports was horse racing. Only gentlemen were allowed to race (and to gamble on the outcome), but anyone could watch. And while men of all ranks throughout the colonies hunted for food,

After a day's work, colonial men often gathered in the local tavern to relax, visit, and discuss current events.

Virginia colonists also hunted just for sport. Society in Virginia was especially class conscious, and each rank used particular animals for their sport hunting: stags for the wealthiest gentlemen, foxes (which initially had to be imported from England) for lesser gentlemen, rabbits and the like for independent farmers, and birds for the lower classes. Cock fighting, too, was a frequently enjoyed spectacle, with much gambling on which bird would be the victor.

Backcountry settlers liked wrestling, target shooting, and tomahawk throwing. They also played an old form of field hockey, and they held gatherings called "Caledonian games." These were similar to the Highland games held in many places today and can also be seen as an ancestor of modern track-and-field events. There were competitions in caber (log) tossing, dancing, broad jump, high jump, a one-mile race, hammer throwing, and shot put—as well as three-legged races, sack races, and wheelbarrow races.

Many colonists also enjoyed games such as cards, dice, backgammon, checkers, billiards, and early forms of bowling. Puritans and Quakers disapproved of most of these because people usually gambled on them. Game playing and gambling often occurred in taverns, which were favorite gathering places. Men—and occasionally women—went there to share drink and conversation with friends. They could also get news of other places from travelers who might have stopped in for a drink, meal, or rest. Men commonly met in taverns to conduct business, too, and even law courts and legislative committees might meet in them.

Boston, New York, and Philadelphia had numerous inns and taverns, of all sizes and catering to all levels of society. In a less-urban area, the local tavern might be a single room in someone's home. Customers would sit together at one table, drinking out of pewter tankards or, sometimes, all sharing the same drinking bowl. Often there was only one room for overnight guests, and travelers, even if they were strangers, would have to share that, too. Large or small, though, taverns (and, in Boston, coffeehouses as well) were among the most important social centers in the colonies.

Men enjoy a selection of newspapers in a library's reading room. Most libraries in the colonies were only for paying subscribers or members. Records show that women used these libraries almost as much as men, and that fiction was borrowed more often than any other type of reading material.

Literature

Colonists who were literate might spend at least some of their leisure time reading. For many, their only (and certainly most important) reading material would have been the Bible, books of sermons, and other religious writings. The well educated often turned to the works of ancient Roman authors, which they frequently read in the original Latin. (Many of these writings, especially by the statesman and philosopher Cicero, had a strong impact on the Founding Fathers.)

During the eighteenth century, colonial newspapers gained more and more readers. There were four newspapers published in the British colonies in 1725, twelve in 1750, and forty-eight in 1775. Another popular publication was the almanac, an annual book that gave the moon phases, tides, weather forecasts, and a calendar for the coming year, and also contained recipes, home remedies, essays, advice,

Enjoying the Arts ❧

In the early years of the colonies, there was little opportunity to enjoy art, concerts, or theater. But in time the arts became a source of pleasure and recreation for many colonists, especially in the middle and upper classes. In the early 1700s artists from Sweden, England, Switzerland, and Germany came to British North America and made at least part of their living by painting portraits of wealthy and important colonists. American-born painters also began to flourish, and around the middle of the century three emerged who became truly great artists: John Singleton Copley, Benjamin West, and Charles Willson Peale. At the same time, there were also many amateur artists in the colonies—folk painters, embroiderers, and others who created portraits and other works for the common people.

Music was part of life at every level of society, and native, European, and African musical traditions were all alive in the Americas. There were work songs, hymns and other religious music, dance tunes, and ballads that told stories in song. For the most part, people made their own music, singing and playing for themselves, their families, and their neighbors, sometimes joining church or community choirs. In the 1700s city dwellers started cultivating a more "refined" lifestyle, as in Europe. Concerts and recitals by professional musicians became increasingly common, and most well-to-do families owned a harpsichord or other small keyboard for family members and guests to play.

Theater took longer than music to become a part of North American culture. As early as 1526, however, Spanish priests were producing religious plays as part of their efforts to convert the native peoples to Christianity. French priests in Canada did the same in the 1600s. The first play known to be staged in the British colonies was performed in a Virginia tavern in 1665—this was a play for entertainment, not religious purposes. Gradually, more nonreligious plays came to be performed in the colonies, sometimes by local amateur groups and sometimes by professional acting companies from Europe. Before long, colonial playgoers were able to enjoy the same dramas and comedies that had become popular in London and Paris.

In British North America the favorite playwright by far was William Shakespeare, whose plays enjoyed nearly 500 performances between 1730 and 1775. During this period, too, colonial entrepreneurs began to build permanent playhouses, and acting companies began to stage professional productions of plays by American authors, such as Massachusetts writer Mercy Otis Warren. Some religious and city authorities frowned on plays as immoral or a waste of time, but the theater was already well on its way to its long reign as a favorite form of American entertainment.

and wise or witty sayings. *Poor Richard's Almanack*, written and published by Benjamin Franklin from 1732 to 1758, was one of the colonies' best sellers.

Fiction had a harder time finding popularity. Puritans (and, to a lesser degree, Quakers) strongly disapproved of fiction because it depended on the imagination rather than on "truth" and because fiction writers put themselves in the place of God by creating worlds of their own in their stories. Besides, in the opinion of Puritan authorities, fiction did not teach anything useful, so reading it was a waste of time. Nevertheless, many colonists did enjoy the English novels of the period, among them *Gulliver's Travels*, by Jonathan Swift, and *Robinson Crusoe*, by Daniel Defoe. It would be some time, though, before North America had any notable novelists of its own.

On the other hand, colonists were not only reading poetry from their homelands but producing poetry of their own almost from the beginning. The first book of poetry written by a British colonist was a collection by Anne Bradstreet, published in London in 1650 as *The Tenth Muse Lately Sprung Up in America*. Many other colonial poems were never printed, but handwritten copies were often passed around and read by groups of friends.

In fact, literary expression was an important part of life for numerous colonists, whether in poems, letters, or diaries and journals. Colonists also wrote histories and descriptions of the New World and their experiences there. One example is William Bradford's *Of Plymouth Plantation*, the original telling of the Pilgrims' story by one of their leaders, which he began writing in 1630 and worked on for the next twenty years.

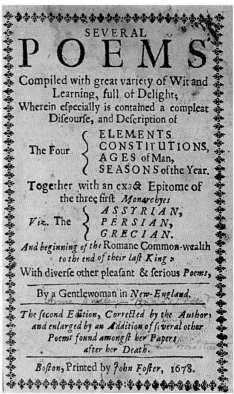

This is the title page of Anne Bradstreet's second collection of poetry. The book contained some of her finest work, including poems about nature, love, family concerns, and life in the New World.

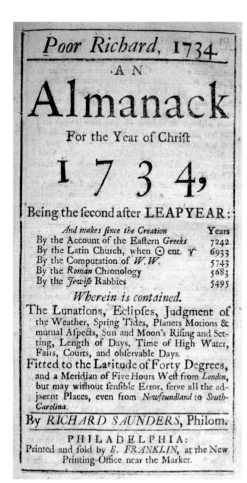

The front cover of Poor Richard's Almanack for the year 1734 advertises the almanac's contents, including the dates of fairs, court sessions, and holidays, and information about such natural events as moon phases, eclipses, and tides.

Special Occasions

Holidays and other special occasions gave colonists a break from their daily routine. Catholic settlers had over a hundred feast days a year. Anglicans had fewer, but many were rich in tradition, especially Christmas. In Virginia, for example, all twelve days from Christmas to January 6 (Twelfth Night) were observed as a season of visiting friends, giving gifts, feasting, and attending parties and dances. Christmas was a major holiday for Dutch colonists, too, who had an array of special breads, cakes, and cookies that they baked just at this time of year.

The Puritans, however, did not believe in celebrating Christmas. In fact, until 1681 the laws of the Massachusetts Bay Colony outlawed it and fined anyone caught feasting, taking the day off from work, or observing the holiday in any other way. Because most English holiday customs were nonbiblical, the Puritans believed it was sinful to celebrate any of the traditional festivals. Quakers did not celebrate them either, but their reasoning was that every day was equally holy, so it seemed wrong to make some days more important than others.

But for most colonists—even Puritans—there were days that were more special than others. Fairs, election days, town meetings, weddings, and funerals were all times when families and communities left off work and joined together, whether in celebration or for some serious purpose—or a little of both. Upper-class Virginia families often made their own occasions. The arrival of an unexpected visitor, for example, might be an excuse to invite the entire neighborhood to a feast. Virginians also loved to give and attend dances, and gentlemen's children spent long hours at dancing lessons to prepare for them.

A Traveler in a Tavern ❧

In 1704 Sarah Kemble Knight, who ran a writing school in Boston, traveled from her home to New York City on business. During her trip she kept a journal of her experiences, including this visit to a Connecticut tavern:

Being come to Mr. Havens', I was very civilly received, and courteously entertained, in a clean comfortable house; and the good woman was very active in helping off my riding clothes, and then asked what I would eat. I told her I had some chocolate, if she would prepare it; which with the help of some milk, and a little clean brass kettle, she soon effected to my satisfaction. I then betook me to my apartment, which was a little room parted from the kitchen by a single board partition; where, after I had noted the occurrences of the past day, I went to bed, which, though pretty hard, [was] yet neat and handsome. But I could get no sleep, because of the clamor of some of the town topers [drunks] in next room, who were entered into a strong debate concerning the signification of the name of their country, . . . Narragansett. One said it was named so by the Indians, because there grew a brier there, of a prodigious height and bigness, the like hardly ever known, called by the Indians Narragansett. . . . His antagonist replied no . . . with a thousand impertinences not worth notice, which he uttered with such a roaring voice and thundering blows with the fist of wickedness on the table, that it pierced my very head. I heartily fretted, and wished him tongue-tied. . . . I set my candle on a chest by the bedside, and sitting up, fell to my old way of composing my resentments, in the following manner:

> I ask thy aid, O potent rum!
> To charm these wrangling topers dumb.
> Thou hast their giddy brains possessed—
> The man confounded with the beast—
> And I, poor I, can get no rest.
> Intoxicate them with thy fumes:
> O still their tongues till morning comes!

And I know not but my wishes took effect, for the dispute soon ended . . . ; and so good night!

The people of Plymouth are shown making their way to their newly built church.

In the winter of 1630–1631, the settlers of Massachusetts Bay were on the brink of starvation. But on February 22, they were saved by the arrival of ships bringing fresh provisions from England. The colony's leaders declared a special day dedicated to giving thanks to God for their deliverance. In the following decades, Puritans held thanksgiving days whenever they felt that God had been especially good to them.

By 1676 Thanksgiving was an annual holiday in New England, celebrated on a Thursday in either November or December. The Puritans marked this occasion with a family dinner, with a fast both before and after. Perhaps the fasts helped them to be all the more grateful for the opportunity to share a bountiful meal with those they loved. In any case, their Thanksgiving holiday has spread and endured to the present, a lasting reminder of the rich legacies of colonial life.

Timeline ‿

Glossary ❧

adobe	Bricks formed of mud and straw then dried in the sun; used as a building material.
Catholic	A Christian who accepts the authority of the pope, the clergy under him, and their teachings.
Church of England	England's state church, headed by the monarch; also known as the Anglican Church. A Protestant church founded by Henry VIII, it was strengthened by his daughter Elizabeth I in the 1500s. It kept the structure of bishops and some practices of the Catholic Church, such as elaborate worship services.
conquistadores	Spanish explorers and conquerors in North and South America.
Enlightenment	A European intellectual movement of the seventeenth and eighteenth centuries. In science and philosophy it promoted observation, experiment, and reason; in politics it promoted freedom, tolerance, and the rights of individuals. Important figures of the Enlightenment included Voltaire and Jean-Jacques Rousseau in France; Sir Isaac Newton, John Locke, David Hume, and Adam Smith in Great Britain; and Thomas Jefferson, John Adams, and Benjamin Franklin in America.
indenture	A contract that bound a person to work for a master for a set period, generally from four to seven years. A person bound by such a contract was called an indentured servant. Sometimes apprentices, too, were bound by indentures.
magistrate	An official who makes sure that laws are enforced and acts as a justice of the peace or judge.
malaria	A disease carried by mosquitoes that causes recurring chills, fevers, and other flu-like symptoms, often leading to death.
midwife	A medical practitioner, usually a woman, who delivers babies and may provide other health care services for women.
militia	A locally based armed force made up of regular citizens (as opposed to professional soldiers). In the English colonies, all able-bodied free males aged sixteen to sixty were summoned to regular "muster days" to practice military drills (and socialize). If the community was attacked, the militia was expected to defend it.
mission	A settlement, usually built around a church and school, established to convert people in the area to Christianity.
missionary	Someone who works to convert people to a new religion.
pioneers	The first settlers of a region.

Protestant	A Christian who rejects the authority of the pope and many other Catholic beliefs.
Puritan	A Protestant who wanted to purify the Church of England, living and worshipping simply and strictly according to the Bible.
Quaker	A member of the Religious Society of Friends, founded in England in the 1600s, which teaches that God works in individuals through an Inner Light. Colonial Quakers promoted nonviolence, tolerance, plain living, and greater equality between women and men and between social classes.
staple	A food that people depend on and eat almost every day, on its own or as a main ingredient in other foods.

Primary Source List ❧

Chapter 1	**p. 17** "The Trappan'd Maiden" from *Albion's Seed: Four British Folkways in America* by David Hackett Fischer, p. 229. New York: Oxford University Press, 1989.
	p. 18 Phillis Wheatley from *Poems on Various Subjects, Religious and Moral,* originally published in 1773. Online at http://www.gutenberg.org/dirs/etext96/whtly10.txt.
Chapter 2	**p. 22** Anne Bradstreet from *The Norton Anthology of Literature by Women: The Tradition in English*, edited by Sandra M. Gilbert and Susan Gubar, p. 69. New York: W.W. Norton, 1985.
	p. 29 John Jones from *Albion's Seed: Four British Folkways in America*, by David Hackett Fischer, p. 468. New York: Oxford University Press, 1989.
Chapter 3	**p. 38** John Ten Broeck from *Child Life in Colonial Days,* by Alice Morse Earl, p. 80–81. 1899. Reprint, Stockbridge, MA: Berkshire House, 1993. Spelling and capitalization modernized.
Chapter 4	**p. 49** Haudenosaunee diplomat and Jolicoeur Charles Bonin from *Daily Life on the Old Colonial Frontier,* by James M. Volo and Dorothy Denneen Volo, p. 37, 86. Westport, CT: Greenwood Press, 2002.
Chapter 6	**p. 73** Abigail Foote from *Home Life in Colonial Days,* by Alice Morse Earl, p. 253. 1898. Reprint, Stockbridge, MA: Berkshire House, 1993.
Chapter 7	**p. 89** Sarah Kemble Knight from "The Journal of Madam Knight." In *Colonial America: An Encyclopedia of Social, Political, Cultural, and Economic History,* edited by James Ciment, p. 1177. Vol. 5. Armonk, NY: M.E. Sharpe, 2006. Spelling and capitalization modernized.

For More Information ≈

The books and Web sites listed below contain information about daily life in colonial America. Most of the books were written especially for young adults. The others will not be too difficult for most young readers. The Web site addresses were accurate when this book was written, but remember that sites and their addresses change frequently. Your librarian can help you find additional resources.

Books

Ciment, James, ed. *Colonial America: An Encyclopedia of Social, Political, Cultural, and Economic History.* 5 vols. Armonk, NY: M.E. Sharpe, 2006.

Colonial America. 10 vols. Danbury, CT: Grolier Educational, 1998.

Dean, Ruth, and Melissa Thomson. *Life in the American Colonies.* San Diego, CA: Lucent Books, 1999.

Fisher, Leonard Everett. *Colonial Craftsmen.* 18 vols. New York: Benchmark Books, 1997, 1998, 1999, 2000.

Hakim, Joy. *A History of Us: Making Thirteen Colonies, 1600–1740.* 2nd ed. New York: Oxford University Press, 1999.

Kalman, Bobbie. *Colonial Life.* New York: Crabtree, 1992.

Kent, Deborah. *How We Lived in Colonial New England.* New York: Benchmark Books, 1999.

———. *How We Lived in the Middle Colonies.* New York: Benchmark Books, 1999.

———. *How We Lived in the Southern Colonies.* New York: Benchmark Books, 1999.

Smith, Carter, ed. *Daily Life: A Sourcebook on Colonial America.* Brookfield, CT: Millbrook Press, 1991.

Stefoff, Rebecca. *American Voices from Colonial Life.* New York: Benchmark Books, 2003.

Warner, John F. *Colonial American Home Life.* New York: Franklin Watts, 1993.

Web Sites

http://www.ci.st-augustine.fl.us/visitors/history.html

A history of St. Augustine, Florida. This site includes a timeline of different periods in the city's history.

http://www.jamestown1607.org/home.asp

This site tells the stories of many of the people who lived in Jamestown, Virginia, around the time it was founded.

http://www.history.org/history/

The Colonial Williamsburg Foundation site contains useful information on how different groups of people lived during the early days of colonial America, and it includes some interesting activities.

http://www.plimoth.org/learn/

The Plimoth Plantation site has information on life in colonial Plymouth, Massachusetts.

http://memorialhall.mass.edu/home.html

Memorial Hall Museum offers activities, information, and online exhibits of objects that were part of daily life in colonial New England.

http://www.chateauramezay.qc.ca/jardin/eng/index.htm

The Web site of the Château Ramezay Museum provides information about Native American agriculture along with photographs and descriptions of the kinds of plants and gardens grown by French colonists in Canada.

http://home.wi.rr.com/rickgardiner/primarysources.htm

The American Colonist's Library: A Treasury of Primary Documents contains links to numerous texts relating to life in colonial America, from medieval and early modern European works that influenced the colonists, all the way up through resolutions and pamphlets from the late 1700s.

http://www.americaslibrary.gov/cgi-bin/page.cgi/jb/colonial

This section of "America's Story" from the Library of Congress provides a timeline and links to information about many fascinating people and events of the colonial period.

http://www.socialstudiesforkids.com/subjects/colonialtimes.htm

This Web site has articles on various aspects of life in the colonies, including games, education, and religion.

http://www.pbs.org/wnet/colonialhouse/

This is the web site for the PBS television show *Colonial House*, in which modern-day people live as the early New England colonists did.

Index ❧